Rewriting the Ink

Before, Behind, and Beyond Bars

Jesse Avina, Michael Lucero,
Frank Perez, Joseph Scheinuck

Edited by Leslie A. Willis

Published by: Leslie A. Willis
Location: San Diego, California, USA
Cover design: Leslie A. Willis
Cover photographs: Leslie A. Willis
Photographs of Authors: Leslie A. Willis
Logo: Rise Up Industries

WritingAfterLife@gmail.com

Copyright © 2023 Leslie A. Willis

All rights reserved. No part of this book may be reproduced or transmitted in any form whatsoever, except in the case of brief quotations in critical reviews or articles, without written permission from the publisher.

Printed in the United States of America
First printing, 2023

ISBN-13: 9798858969907

The stories told in this book are the reflections of the authors on their own lives and are not meant to represent the experiences of all justice-involved individuals. These stories do not represent the opinions or viewpoints of Rise Up Industries.

The publisher is donating one hundred percent of the net proceeds of this book to Rise Up Industries.

Table of Contents

Foreword 1
Introduction 4

Michael Lucero 13

Childhood or a War Zone 14
Just Trying to Survive 21
1999, The Year I Lost Everything 29
I Owe It to More Than Myself 37
New Life, New Challenges 43

Frank Perez 55

Survival Mode 56
A Mother's Bond 60
Prison: Life Continued 65
A New Life Sentence 71

Jesse Avina 81

A Message to a Child 82
Finding a Home on the Streets 86
The Beginning of Two Different Worlds 91
Leaving My Comfort Zone 96
Trying Something New 101

Joseph Scheinuck 109

Introduction 110
An Old Boy 112
A Troubled Man 119
A Kind God 126
Freedom on the Outside 132
Conclusion 138

Afterword 141
Book Discussion Questions 147
Resources 151
Acknowledgments 153
About the Project 157
A Word from the Founder of Rise Up
    Industries 159

Foreword
Ernie Garcia

When asked if I would write this foreword, I was surprised and honored – simply because the first book, *Writing After Life,* which I co-authored with three other ex-lifers, had such an impact on my life. I mean at the time of the first book I was still trying to understand myself in regards to my life as a "free man." As we sat in our meetings on Monday mornings discussing the latest chapter we had written, it always brought me back to issues that I had secreted deep within myself. You have to understand, in prison I was taught to keep things to myself. To reveal as little about myself as possible. And then there I was in the first book sharing all this personal information: my fears, hurts, dreams, faith, and in the end my triumphs.

The impact of the first book was cathartic because for once I saw clearly everything that I had been through, and I knew that my purpose was greater than the thuggish life I had once led. Through the process, I was able to see where I had been and how far I had come, which only convinced me to be more grateful for the miracle, the second chance, that God's grace had given me.

Since the publishing of the first book, I have continued to walk in faith and to be of service to others. I am on the board of directors for In Christ United, LLC, which holds events to raise money for charities that care for children with cancer, battered women, victims of sex trafficking, and the homeless. A couple times a year, I travel to Ensenada, Mexico, to bring food and clothing to the children of the camps/campos who work in the farming fields. I work in distribution, and I'm working toward establishing my own LLC. I am also the proud stepfather of a 12-year-old.

My passion will remain in trying to make a difference in this world, one step at a time. I continue to be a guest speaker at high schools and other events where I feel my voice may help others see the slippery slope of bad choices and the heartwarming blessing of redemption.

The gentlemen in this second book – Mike, Frank, Jesse, and Joe – each have a very powerful story. These stories are impactful because they are true, and real. Their stories allow us to see a part of their soul, a part of them that shows vulnerability - which is very difficult for anyone, let alone someone who has done serious time. These stories allow us to see that we don't have to be defined by our past transgressions, but that we can rebuild and remake the individuals we were into the individuals that we were meant to be.

I am very proud of these gentlemen. It takes commitment and hard work to complete a project like this because it can be mentally and emotionally draining. It also takes a certain amount of bravery to write honestly about one's life, and I am grateful for their courage to speak their truth. I know their stories will have a positive impact on the lives of others for as long as people choose to read.

It is great that Rise Up decided to support a second book. I know that the overall message in this book is universal: We can change. We can do better. We can be better. We have all been hurt. We have all faced adversity and have been left with scars. Yet, through these stories, we understand healing comes from seeing beyond ourselves and embracing empathy and compassion for others.

Introduction
Leslie A. Willis

"Have you considered writing another book?" Jonathan, the Deputy Executive Director of Rise Up Industries, asked. "The response to the first one has been really positive."

This wasn't the first time I had been asked about writing a second book, yet this time, it felt different. This time, the timing felt possible. Most aspects of everyday life had returned to "normal" since the onset of COVID-19, time in my schedule was opening up, and I was looking for a meaningful way to re-engage in my community. When there also seemed to be considerable interest from the current members at Rise Up Industries, it felt like the perfect fit.

In 2018, I co-created a program with four members of Rise Up Industries' Reentry Program, who had all been recently released from prison, to share their stories and change perceptions surrounding individuals who have experienced incarceration. This project culminated in the publication of a book, *Writing After Life: Stories from Those Who Served a Life Sentence*.

Since *Writing After Life* was published, it has been read across the country in prisons, juvenile halls, book clubs, classrooms, and religious organizations, even book clubs in prisons and in juvenile halls. We've received dozens of letters and emails from prison residents, Rise Up Industries donors, and religious leaders thanking us for sharing these stories and offering hope and proof of change. One of the authors had been a participant in a Buddhist Foundation's prison outreach correspondence program prior to his release. After reading the book, the Foundation ordered 1,200 books that they sent across the country to prison residents on their mailing list.

In January 2023, I sat down with a new group of Rise Up Industries members to discuss the possibility of writing a book that would feature their stories. Over the next couple weeks, we discussed our goals, our hesitations, and our excitements regarding a new book project.

Together, we developed a plan. We would structure the new book similar to the first and include stories from pivotal times in their lives – childhood, adolescence, prison, and re-entry. I would guide the process and support their progress, offering prompts and suggestions every step of the way.

And thus, the writing began.

Five years ago, the table in the Rise Up Industries conference room was covered with piles of lined paper, whole sections crossed out and rewritten as pens ran out of ink and pencil tips broke. Several individuals scribbled away, writing their stories with pen and paper before making the final edits on the old big boxy desktop computers.

Now, that same table is weighted with multiple open laptops. The sounds of clicking keyboards filled the conference room as four new authors typed away, writing their life stories. It hasn't been easy; revisiting and retelling some of the toughest and most emotionally difficult experiences in one's life never is. At times, emotions ran high, tears were shed, and deep breaths were taken in order to keep working.

But the belief in the importance of sharing their experiences and their messages in the hopes that they will positively impact others, even just one person, was enough to keep them going.

Throughout the seven months we have been writing together, deep self-discoveries have been made, aha moments have occurred, and bonds between the authors have been strengthened as they gave support and encouragement to each other. The conversations and reflections have continued far beyond the one and a half to six hours we shared together each week.

*****

There is power in writing and telling our stories.

We write our stories to process our experiences. In allowing ourselves to slow down and reflect on our lived experiences, we can begin to understand ourselves in a deeper way. We can process our feelings – both pleasant and challenging – associated with those experiences, understand our thought patterns, and acknowledge the impacts of our actions.

We write our stories to heal. Through writing and processing our traumatic and challenging experiences in a structured environment, we can gain perspective that enables us to differentiate the core of who we are from those harmful events that have happened to us. After all, hurt people hurt people, and there is healing in realizing that we are much more than our past actions. We accept that our past experiences are part of who we are, yet they do not define who we have the potential to be.

We write our stories to connect. By sharing our stories with others, we build bridges of empathy, compassion, and connection with people we know and love, and with strangers we may never meet. We realize our experiences are not unique to us, that we are inextricably linked to others. No one is alone, and through our stories, we bring to light our common humanity and shared experiences.

We write our stories to break the cycle. Through revealing our truths and the lessons we've learned along the way, we plant seeds of redirection for others traveling down a dangerous path, misguided by their own past experiences, intergenerational traumas, and negative societal pressures. We can create greater understanding regarding the root causes that lead to cycles of violence, incarceration, recidivism, and other societal harms - and work to break the cycles.

We write our stories to bring awareness to society's injustices. We do not all start life on a level playing field. Social structures privilege certain groups and marginalize others, creating conditions in which individuals may not have sufficient choices. It is through exposure, education, and reflection that we can understand and acknowledge the inequities of the society in which we live - and offer solutions to build a more just world.

We write our stories to inspire action. When we experience the personal and emotional connections that stories offer, they can move us into action - to engage, to volunteer, to advocate, or to support in numerous other ways individuals or social causes we believe in. We may discover new causes and feel called to action. Stories have the power to change our behaviors as we make greater meaning of the world around us and our role in it.

And in sharing our stories, we give permission to others to share theirs. It is through such mutual sharing that we learn about ourselves, develop empathy for others, and begin to make and deepen our connections to ourselves, each other, and the world. By embracing the vulnerability to share our stories, we can support others to find the courage to do so as well, expanding the reach of healing and transformation that storytelling offers.

*****

We have titled this book *Rewriting the Ink* because, while the tattoos on the authors' bodies tell one story, the authors are taking back their lives by owning how their stories are told and telling a more complete story. These stories tell not only of what they did – actions they no longer condone, but also why they did what they did. They touch on how early life environments and mentalities play a role in one's involvement in gangs and criminality, as well as the realities of a life in prison. But they don't stop there.

Rewriting the Ink is also about the possibility of transformation and the ongoing growth that is experienced through making a profound change in one's life; for the authors, this led to their release from prison and the joys and challenges of reintegrating into civil society.

The stories told in these pages contain vivid descriptions of the realities of life, and some truths may be difficult to read. They may resonate with you, our readers, in deep and possibly painful ways. We encourage you to practice self-care as you read these stories and reach out for help from trained professionals, community resources, and other systems of support as needed. We have provided a list of National Hotlines and resources in the back of the book as well.

Our hope in publishing this second book is that we can continue to acknowledge our shared humanity and believe that, first and foremost, we are all human. These are stories that deserve to be heard.

(August 2023)

Editor's Note:

It is important to note that we do not condone or attempt to glorify the authors' past actions, behaviors, or beliefs. We include some details of their crimes to offer contrast between their previous and present mindsets and to reveal how exceptional their transformations have been. Through the process of reflection and story sharing, much respect and acknowledgement has been given to victims and their families, as well as others who have been affected by gang violence, crime, and the criminal justice system.

Rewriting the Ink

Rewriting the Ink

Michael Lucero

Childhood or a War Zone

Looking back now, I still wonder how I am even alive. My father and mother loved to party. Drugs, alcohol, crime, and extreme violence: these were constants in my earliest memories. For years I truly thought all families did drugs, drank all night, and fought. My parents would rage out of control, things would explode around us, there would be holes in walls, broken windows and doors, gunshots exploding outside our windows, and police lights flashing their red, blue, red, blue spiral. My father and family friends would explode into fights of rage. There were so many trips to the emergency room with my mom being hurt – broken nose, bloody lips, and black eyes that were too often empty and hopeless.

My heart would pump so hard and fast at times! My little brother Jon would often cling to me scared and needing comfort. We were only sixteen months apart in age, and we were inseparable.

This was the first ten years of my life.

One time, when I was nine years old, my mom got us away. We were living with my grandparents, playing baseball, in school, and happy. I was so glad it was just us - Mom, Jon, and me. Then one day I came home from school, and my mom very awkwardly tried to tell me she had a surprise.

"Dad's coming home, and he's taking us to Delaware," she said. I was crushed, like I'd been punched in the stomach. *Everything was good again, so why?* This was the first time I thought, *No, it won't work*.

And it didn't. The following year I saw my dad abuse my mom more than ever. My mom tried to escape it in the only way she knew how: making friends close by that had the same interests of drugs, partying, and too much drinking. But it was out of control. One early morning after my dad had beat my mom in front of us, she put Jon and me in the truck and said to us, "This is done. I am so sorry I did this."

"I told you this would happen," I replied.

We drove to the courthouse and police station, scared and nervous with everything seeming very surreal. I can still remember the man we talked to saying, "We will go take him out of the house right now, but can you keep yourself from letting him come back?" My mom paused, shifting back and forth on the balls of her feet. She was crying and looked over at us as we sat there, my little brother crying. She turned to him and said, "I promise, never again."

That was a fact! Never again did my mom let my dad back to live with us.

It was just us three now. With no job skills and not sure what we'd do or how we'd eat, my mom bravely took a stand to change her and her children's lives once and for all. She finally realized if she did not, someone would be dead - more than likely herself!

Little did I know the journey didn't stop here; it was only just beginning. Years of abuse and drug and alcohol dependency began to fuel the anger, confusion, and misdirection that now possessed our family.

My mom soon found work driving school buses, and we tried to go to school like normal. The new problem was that my mom could now drink and use more freely with her friends since she didn't have to worry about my dad controlling her anymore. We'd gotten rid of one problem – my dad – but not yet dealt with the others. She hadn't learned how to live without the person who both hurt us the most and also took care of us.

My dad would call and make hours of late-night promises. Once or twice I'd hear him knock, but my mom very bravely stood her ground. She was struggling with how to take care of two young boys and be brave and productive all at the same time.

I began to really struggle in school. I couldn't concentrate or do what was asked. I was deeply worried that my mom would allow him to come back home, so I was constantly thinking of how to get myself and my younger brother away if that happened. It was winter, and the bus stop was a good walk away. Then there was a long 45-minute bus ride to school. I began intentionally missing the bus and days at school.

With my mom now working, she didn't know I was skipping class. The school, however, became worried. A nice counselor would try to talk to me, but too much emotion would well up and I'd run from her. Because I was missing from class all the time, my classmates often picked on me. I didn't like this, and all that I was going through began to come out in rage. I soon got into fights at school almost every day.

My school recommended a temporary stay at a school for Seriously Emotionally Disturbed Children. I liked it and it also meant that I got home earlier, which meant less supervision and more freedom to do what I wanted. My mom drank a lot during this time, missed work, and at times did not make it home at all. I'd stay up worrying, feeding my little brother, and feeling increasing resentment toward her. One night she came home drunk and so mad at something that she got very physical with me, more than any other time. The neighbors intervened and took me to sleep in their home for the night. I lay crying on their living room floor in a sleeping bag, missing my little brother.

Over the next few days, my mom kept raging out of control at me for one thing or another. I realized she was beginning to do to me what my dad would do to her. I wasn't going to let this start happening to me, too. I'd had enough - not just with my mom's behavior, but all of it: being hurt and hating how I was treated, especially by someone I loved so deeply!

I was at a breaking point. I remember fighting – at school, in my apartment complex, and at times with my younger brother – and always feeling better afterwards. One time, my mom began yelling and screaming at me while I was in the kitchen. I got scared because her yelling always led to more and I'd had enough. Suddenly, I felt all hot and overwhelmed. I grabbed a glass bowl and slung it at the ground, screaming "Stop!" She grew angrier so I kept going. I was breathing hard, grabbing anything I could and throwing it at the floor, yelling louder and louder.

All of a sudden, it grew quiet. Everything stopped. I looked up. My mom was gone and all around me was a pile of broken dishes. I panted hard, suddenly realizing just how scared and sad I was.

I loved my mom and never wanted this to happen between us. I felt like my dad – acting out in rage and anger and creating catastrophe myself. I began to cry as I started picking up the broken glass. It cut my fingers and my hand started to bleed. My mom appeared with our neighbors. They pleaded for me to stop, walking carefully through the glass to get to me. They told me it was alright and led me into my bedroom. My mom was crying and saying, "I love you, I'm sorry," as she wiped the blood from my hands. I was sorry, too.

She then told me she had called the phone number the new behavioral school gave her in case of emergencies. I didn't know what that meant, but soon I heard a knock at the door and two big adults walked in. My mom went to talk with them while I sat there holding the towel in my hand to stop the bleeding like she showed me. I knew we'd be ok; I loved my mom and she always fixed things.

Then the two people came in and sat very close on both sides of me. I felt them each wrap their hands around my arms before explaining that they were going to take me to a safe place so things could cool off at home.

I began to cry. "Please don't let them take me. Mom, I'm sorry!" I pleaded.

She kept telling me it was only for the night, so I'd get help. I was hurt and felt I had ruined everything. Now my dad and I were both taken, and I felt so sad that I may have made my mom feel the same way my dad had made her feel for so many years.

The two adults walked me out of the house, put me in a car with a cage between us, and drove off. The red emergency light on the dashboard flashed as it spun. They were silent. I had no clue where we were going, and I had no idea this would begin a pattern that would last for 35 years.

Just Trying to Survive

Throughout all of these changes in my school and home, I just wanted to be a normal kid who fit in. My mom, brother, and I were moving around so much after my parents separated that I didn't have many friends or stability. School was always easy for me but I never really took part in all the social activities, like going to other kids' birthday parties, school events, or anything that cost money. I knew money was hard for my mom, being a single mother and trying to do it all on her own, so I just wouldn't ask about it.

Around the age of 10, I began to struggle in school with other kids. I'd fight in class and just ignore authority. Soon the school stepped in, suggesting to my mom that I had an anger problem and poor impulse control. They had me start talking to a psychiatrist. Soon they had me try multiple medications and admitted me to psychiatric centers for treatment.

These places only made me sadder and more confused. Each time I went in for treatment, they would send me through a battery of tests, counseling, and more medications, all of which just brought more confusion. I became angrier and more impulsive. I didn't understand. All I wanted was to be home and happy, but they – my mom, the authorities, the social workers, and child services – wouldn't let me go home. I felt hopeless. No matter what I did, there seemed to be no real path to go home and be able to stay there, so I stopped cooperating. Over the next few years, I passed through every hospital and long-term placement there was in San Diego.

By the age of 13, I'd begun to drink regularly, smoke marijuana, and had tried coke and meth. I was quickly on my way to becoming an addict. I realized I found more love and acceptance with my friends than with my own family. My mom seemed to hate me and anything and everything I did or said. She was working on her own recovery and raising me added to her challenges. Honestly, I feel the system influenced her to believe that these placements were the best thing for me. Even when I'd share what would happen there – physical abuse, neglect, and sadly, sexual abuse as well – nothing seemed to deter her from insisting I be put away, far from home.

I would run away from the treatment center, go back home or to a friend's house for a bit, before ending up in another placement facility. One time I ran away from my mom's to my friend John's. We drank, partied, and hung out with the neighborhood kids. The next thing I remember is waking up in a field late at night. I'd thrown up, passed out, and wasn't sure where anyone was.

I began walking just to get my bearings. I got sick again. This time, it scared me. I was throwing up blood – a lot of it. I wiped my mouth and found my way to a pay phone. I swallowed my pride and called my mom collect to have her help me and explain the blood and sickness I was experiencing. She accepted, sounding relieved to hear from me, yet also upset. I told her I was sick, my stomach hurt, and I kept throwing up blood. She told me I'd be ok, that she was on her way. I felt somewhat assured.

Why can't she always be like this, wanting me home and willing to overlook challenges to make sure I'm ok?, I thought. I loved my mom with all my heart, but had grown very confused from what our relationship had turned into.

I sat on the curb, my stomach heaving. I leaned to the side to get sick again. More blood. I knew my mom would be here soon. She'd know what to do, and I'd be ok. I watched the parking lot for her car. As I looked back and forth, I was startled by the two police cars that entered the parking lot and quickly pulled up in front of me. Both spotlights were pointed directly at me. I put my hands up to protect my eyes, then looked away to act as if maybe they'd see I wasn't who they were looking for.

Yet, they both got out quickly. "Are you Michael?", one of them asked as he walked towards me.

The other officer circled around me, grabbed the back of my arm tightly, and yanked me off the ground. I winced and told them to chill. But they pressed my face down onto the hood of the car and cuffed my hands. When they searched me, they found a switchblade knife in my pocket. I thought nothing of it. I'd taken it from my grandfather who had cool knives and stuff. I'd always liked it and thought I may need it when running away. I didn't know there were laws against this type of knife in California.

They explained how my mom called and told them I had run away and broken into a relative's house (which I had done just to sleep).

Of course she would call the cops, I thought.

The officers took me to the hospital since I was still throwing up blood. The doctor said I had an ulcer of sorts, which wasn't good for a 13-year-old to have, and prescribed me some medications. I remember he told the officers how often I was to take the medication, but they dismissed him saying, "He'll be home. His mother can deal with it."

Optimistically, I asked them if I was going home. They said they were booking me in on the weapons charge, but the Halls would call my mom to come get me.

I laughed and shook my head, "My mom won't pick me up. She called you." I knew that if she was going to pick me up, she would have already.

They booked me into Juvenile Hall, printed me, took pictures, and called my mom. Eventually they came in and explained that if she didn't come, they'd have to hold me. I'd be considered abandoned and housed there. There was no one else I could call. I knew calling my dad would only make matters worse.

A guard escorted me into a unit of other boys, carrying my bed roll. Honestly, I was kinda nervous. In all the placements I'd been in, I heard a lot of bad things about Juvie: fights, gangs, drama, stuff that no one really wants to deal with. I walked by one unit and thought, *Oh man, these guys are huge and got freaking tattoos on their faces!* Then we entered another unit, and everyone was much smaller – my size. *Much better*, I thought, relieved.

This stay began a whole series of stays through my adolescence. It was in Juvenile Hall that I began to identify with the guys I knew from my neighborhood and school. Our entire group was in and out nonstop. I became more involved with this group each time I was released. Before I knew it, I was following them into fights and gang initiations. The day I got jumped into the gang felt like an honorable thing. I was told "We are your family, we will never leave you, abandon you, or ever let anyone hurt you." This was exactly what I was looking for in my childhood from my own family.

It's weird how that works, I don't think anyone joins a gang to be part of an organized group of criminals. We are mostly looking for the sense of family that so many of us often didn't have a healthy version of growing up. What used to get us punished – things like fighting, getting in trouble, and being rebellious – were celebrated and rewarded by this family. This wasn't a productive thing for a lost lonely kid with a lot of anger and confusion in his heart and mind.

After I joined the gang, I'd get in trouble much more often, each time with growing severity. Probation officers would come looking for me, and I'd run and hide. We all did. Eventually I would get arrested, go through the court and Juvenile Hall process, and then be sent to a placement, group home, or foster home.

In these places, I would continue to represent this new family, forcing my dominance by violence. Thus, my reputation would grow. Knowing who's who and who did what was huge in there. I'd take pride in the fact that my reputation would actually cause others to avoid me. I used to fight a lot. Any opportunity to fight was an opportunity to build my rep and get a vacation, so I'd be the first to jump and get there quickly. Today, I can look back and see how dysfunctional this caused me to be in life. It took many decades to correct.

After fighting, I would be placed in my cell, alone, nice and quiet, where I could read for days nonstop. Reading was a new thing I discovered inside. I came to love reading. I would read Aristotle, Plato, classics, fiction and nonfiction, self-help books, economics, religious books – anything I could get my hands on.

Soon I ran out of places to be sent. I was told upon my release from a juvenile detention camp, after close to a year this time, that upon any more arrests I'd be sent to California Youth Authority (CYA).

I got out and didn't even really try to succeed. I only made it 35 days before being re-arrested for two assaults with deadly weapons and gun charges. I knew I was facing a lot more time.

1999, The Year I Lost Everything

1999 was the worst year of my life! All these years later, I'm still plagued by it and all that I lost back then.

Out on parole, only twenty years old, and in the chaos my life had come to, I wondered what was coming next. After serving multiple years in the California Youth Authority, I was finally home again. I tried going to school and holding down a job, but that didn't last long. My younger brother needed help so I quit school and my job to help him – not the things one should do, but I thought that if I was back in the neighborhood with him, I could watch over him like I should have been doing all along. Struggling, on heroin, and living with friends, I knew he was headed for destruction.

Trying to help my brother, I quickly found myself being drawn back into the web of addiction and gang culture. Until you learn something new, nothing can just be started anew. Like a glass of water, as the water pours out, the glass fills with air until fluid is poured back in. I wanted to find "the air" to replace the water in my glass of life but didn't know how to fill my life with a new way. So, before I knew it, the old way crept back in.

It was June eighth. I walked into our bedroom at home to check on my little brother only to find him unconscious and turning blue. I quickly called my mom, then called 911, and we gave him CPR until the medics arrived. The bedroom became a whirlwind of chaos – emergency lights flashing, responders moving rapidly, more family members arriving. It all felt surreal while they treated him. My mom prayed and cringed in hope, but I already knew the outcome. My little brother was dead. He had OD'd.

Finally, after a short time, the head firefighter came out of the bedroom. He said they'd tried everything; there was nothing else they could do. My mom broke. She cried holding me. My family gathered, comforting one another. It was devastating. I looked around at everyone's reactions; there was so much sadness.

Exactly five months later, I was in custody again. I'd violated parole and was in a 90-day violators program in El Centro, California. I was headed to my inmate assigned job when they called me into the supervisor's office and sat me down.

Picking up the phone, they called my family. I knew that an unplanned call in custody usually meant bad news. My mom was on the other end. She told me that one of my best friends, his twin brother, and several others had all been shot at the beach the night before. She was at the hospital with Peter who had been shot four times and survived. Our mothers were good friends, and we were all very close. My good friend Paul hadn't made it.

I felt my heart drop and shatter. I was speechless. I couldn't move. So quickly I was experiencing tragedy again. I'd just lost my little brother, and now Paul. They had been there for me through everything I'd just experienced. I couldn't believe one of my best friends was gone so suddenly.

I woke up the next morning still in shock. I couldn't stop thinking about losing my brother and one of my best friends. This was on top of losing another friend the year prior. Death was surrounding me, creeping closer and closer. *Was I next?* I was coming to a realistic understanding that I was headed to either prison or death.

The staff left me alone that day. I stayed in my cell and read and thought. Around 4:30pm I got ready to go work in the kitchen. I saw the staff watching me. As I walked by, they called me over. The sergeant said, "You're going to have a special visit right now. Head to the P.O.'s office."

On the way, I saw the pastor of my family's church, Pastor Bill, walk in. I was excited to see him. My pastor was cool. I really respected and loved him, and felt relieved to have someone I knew come to see me after everything that happened. I figured he had come to check up on me and encourage me after I lost my friend. He'd always been there for me and my family through the good and hard times.

Pastor Bill came in and hugged me. We sat down, and he asked how I'd been. I shared that I was still sad from losing my little brother Jonathan and then Paul so quickly after.

He was quiet, then began to speak.

The night before, after my mom got home from the hospital, my youngest stepbrother, Branden, had been riding his bike home from school when he was struck and killed by another young driver.

I sat there, stunned, having an out of body experience.

In a five-month period, both brothers, blood and step, and a best friend had all been killed. At age 21, this sent me down a spiral of darkness. I tried to run from what I felt building inside me – anger, confusion, and a sense of impending doom that I would be next to die.

Over the next year and a half, I felt directionless. I was in and out of prison. Let out on parole, I was living with a group of my homeboys, drinking, using, and feeling miserable inside. I grew more distant from my friends and family and became more dangerous in my thoughts and behaviors. I tried going to church, and even tried bible college, but I just kept getting drawn back to the gang and neighborhood culture I was so enmeshed in. In times of trouble, I would always go back to doing what I was familiar with, like muscle memory, and with the gang was where I was most comfortable.

One day, I went by my mom and stepdad's house to talk to my mother. I noticed one of my ex-girlfriends living there. I knew this was bad news. She was a drug addict running around doing scandalous stuff, and I didn't want my parents to get caught up in her mess. I warned them and warned them, but instead of listening they told me to stay away.

Sadly, I was right. One day, she stole my parents' best friend's car. But what made me furious was that my parents blamed ME for it. I started to seethe with anger. I was drunk, angry, and still struggling with my own life – looking at everyone else's faults and not my own.

Instead of going straight home that night, I stopped at a pay phone and called my mom, hurt and upset that they thought I'd steal their car. I yelled at her until my stepdad grabbed the phone and argued back at me, defending my mom. I felt enraged and screamed threats at him before hanging up. I turned and drunkenly stumbled to their place to challenge him. Once again, I'd had enough.

Once there, I beat on the door. My stepdad came out and listened to me as I screamed, expressing how I hated how they treated me, felt disrespected, and threatened to hurt him like I felt hurt. Understandably, my stepdad seemed upset, and he stood up to me. But at that time in my life, I didn't allow people to stand up to me.

I pulled out a knife, stabbed my stepdad twice, and ran off yelling in rage. I don't share this with a lot of people. Up until this moment, I saw my stepdad only as mom's husband, not as a father figure. But that night I crossed a line I didn't know was there.

That night, I hurt my own family in a very serious way.

I ran and ran and ran. It took the police almost a year to find me halfway across the United States and living with my older half-brother from my dad's other marriage. I received a four-year prison sentence that thrust me back into the world of gang involvement, incarceration, and addiction. When I was released, I tried to lay low and get back to my half-brother's place, but I wasn't allowed to transfer.

One night, eleven months after I got out, I was with the wrong people and intoxicated with alcohol and drugs. With unprocessed struggles, I offended again. Multiple people were stabbed in a brawl – including one I stabbed multiple times – and severely hurt. I jumped in a car and sped off, knowing I would likely be caught.

It wasn't immediate, but within a few months when I was checking in to take a drug test at my Parole Office, I was cuffed and booked on two counts of attempted murder. I fought this case for close to two years in county jail. I was facing a life sentence plus a ton of years on top of that given my past record. I thought I'd do time; I just wasn't sure how much.

For the first time in my life, all of my parents – my mom, dad, and stepdad – actually worked together and got me an attorney to give me another chance at life. Fortunately for me, my stepdad and I had reconciled after my last prison term. He found it in his heart, through his walk with Christ and his love for my mother, to forgive me for what I did. I felt so undeserving of his forgiveness, and yet his strength to do so gave me hope that one day I could change. Over time, we spent much more time together and became pretty close. This time, as I faced the possibility of a life sentence, he really came to my aid, along with my biological dad and mom. It felt like the first time I had everyone on my side, and I was so grateful, despite ultimately receiving a 17-year sentence.

Once in prison, I realized that, then in my mid-twenties, I was not going to get out until my mid-forties. That was hard to accept. It felt insurmountable. *Was this all my life was going to be? Would I ever be able to break this cycle and stay out for good?*

I Owe It to More Than Myself

During the first few years of my incarceration, I really thought about how I was ever going to make it to the finish line – one day being out of prison alive. That's much easier said than done. I knew it would be difficult to figure out the road map, especially after being in prison for so long.

The last time I had been out, I had gotten in contact with Stevie, a friend of mine who was doing life in prison. We'd been very close growing up. I was also in touch with Joseph, my homeboy and distant cousin. I always had a great deal of respect for these two. Both were spending a lot of time in prison. They'd both made some radical changes in their own lives like disassociating from the gang lifestyle, remaining clean and sober, programming, and changing their message. Not only had they made these changes, thus far they were sustaining them as well, and I knew they were reaping rewards for these changes in many areas.

So this time, I decided to do a few things very different from all the other times I was incarcerated. I eventually disassociated myself from the gang affiliation I always held. This was difficult – prison is not a place you can just say, "Time-out, I'm done with you." There are repercussions for disassociating. I ultimately was able to do so, though. I was glad, but it also left me on my own, still with all the same problems.

I realized a lot of the dysfunction in my life wasn't isolated only to my gang involvement. I had very broken, criminalistic thinking. From the idea that force is a necessity of life in all matters, to always finding ways to manipulate others, viewing people and every relationship as a means to an end. I adapted to the need for survival, but eventually this led to a life plagued by the cycle of incarceration. In addition to that, I knew my drug and alcohol dependency was at the forefront of what I needed to deal with.

I sought out cellies who were trying to work on themselves to learn what I could from them. I knew there was no set way to fix myself and that no one was going to make the change for me. I had to find the right ingredients for myself. I've heard it said,

"You're a monster in a box trying to find the right mix to get yourself right." I pictured a fuzzy monster in a cage with shot glasses for every self-help group, college class, and religion in front of him, wondering why he was still a monster since he was drinking the mix, glass after glass. Yet he was still a fuzzy beast! I was still a fuzzy beast.

So I worked, learned, and tried a few new things. I mean, I tried everything: Narcotics Anonymous, Alcoholics Anonymous, Celebrate Recovery, and Victims Awareness meetings for years and years. I studied CBT, God's Word, and read everything I could get my hands on. I journaled, really reflected on my childhood, and became aware of why I processed life through my mind and heart the way I did.

Naturally, there were some detours along the way. Ending my alcohol and drug use was very hard for me. Drugs were so easy to obtain in prison, I felt like a crackhead in a crack house. *How was I supposed to stay clean and sober?* This took time for me, but I kept getting back up when I'd fall. I would take more classes and stay sober a little longer.

During this time, I also did a couple long-term isolation stays in the SHU (Security Housing Unit) due to violence. In April of 2014, with pins and screws in my hand, another victim hurt, and with hardly any recollection of what happened that night, I realized I could no longer drink. That was the last time I drank. I still took some time to kick the drug addiction, but I kept at it.

Finally, after having a very deep spiritual experience through Kairos Prison Ministry, I found the complete mix I needed. All of the ingredients were in place. It was at Kairos that I really began to identify that my drug habit was deep-seated and would take a lifetime of work to counteract. Working through the 12-steps with my sober brothers in Christ and identifying how, when, and why I truly began to use helped me to overcome some of those reasons why I had remained addicted for so long.

I got involved in the prison's college program as well. As I learned, my thinking began to be restructured and as my thinking changed, so did my behavior. I stayed busy with college, self-help, my walk with Christ, and rebuilding relationships with positive influences in my life.

In the midst of my change, a very close friend of mine, Nicol, reinitiated contact with me and became a very positive support figure for me. Nicol was someone I'd met through friends back in 2001; we even worked together for a brief time. During that time when I was still involved in the gang culture and my addictions, she had recently come out of her own addiction. I greatly admired her for the change she had found back then. But due to my incarceration, we'd lost touch until 2018. Now, we were growing closer and closer than ever before through phone calls, letters, and visitations.

A year after reconnecting, I proposed to Nicol in the prison visiting room, and she said "Yes!" Life began to seem much more positive for me and the potential of my future seemed so much clearer with her by my side.

I began to realize that after being away for so long, around 15 years at this point, I would need assistance in my reentry attempt. I told Nicol and my mom during visits that I wanted to look for a program; I wanted something to help with the transition back into society.

A few months before being released, I received a printout from a social worker with a list of reentry programs. One of the programs had a picture of a group of guys smiling and mentioned Rise Up Industries. I asked someone at Kairos Prison Ministry about it. They had really good things to say about Rise Up, and I was glad to hear that. My fiancée and mom both looked into the organization as well and felt it was an amazing program.

It was only a few miles from the place I would be living. I felt that minimizing my exposure to at-risk influences by keeping my circle small and healthy was necessary and could help me adjust to mainstream society from the extremely structured environment I'd been in so long. Being truly institutionalized is a fear I often dealt with. *Would I be able to function out there?* I thought that Rise Up could be a potential place to support my transition.

I wrote to the director, Joe Gilbreath, and he wrote back to me, inviting me to an interview upon my release. I began to pray over it. I was hopeful and committed to contacting them immediately upon my release, feeling it may be just the change I needed to stay out this time.

Finally, after attaining three associate degrees from my college program and completing my requirements from my welding class trade assignments, I was given a large time cut and released on October 30th, 2021. I couldn't believe I was finally getting another chance.

New Life, New Challenges

In the middle of the pandemic, with Nicol and I literally counting down the days, the day finally came. On October 30th, 2021, several hours after expecting to be processed for release, they finally called my name.

The building erupted with guys yelling their goodbyes through prison doors. I waved and wished them well as I carried my box of pictures, paper work, and my Bible home. I told my cellie Jairo goodbye and that I'd be in contact with him again soon.

After dressing in the clothes my fiancée had purchased for me and doing an hour's worth of paperwork, I was ushered into a van with a young guy who'd just done a year or so.

Fifteen years after entering the prison, I was driven through those prison gates for what I truly hoped would be the last time. My mom and my soon-to-be-wife awaited me, standing by the truck as the prison van pulled over and let me out. I hugged them both as we cried and smiled all together. I couldn't believe this day had finally come, once and for all.

We laughed and talked as my mom drove us straight to Pacific Beach where we met my stepdad. We all ate breakfast together at my family's favorite local place, Kono's.

As soon as we were done, I rode home with my stepdad as my mom and Nicol sped off to get ready. Nicol and I were getting married down at the beach in two hours. My mom had saved up to get me clothes for my wedding day: pretty simple slacks, dress shoes, and a gray button up shirt.

Everything was moving in slow motion, even though time flew by as I took everything in. To see my parents' home again after all these years – the place where my brothers, Jon and Branden, and I once all lived together; the place where my little brother Jon died; the place my stepdad and I had our falling out so many years ago and where, by God's Amazing Grace, he was now so welcoming. It was such a blessing to walk into my parents' home that day in good standing with them, getting ready to marry my best friend and love of my life.

Within a blur of minutes, I stood in the pastor's backyard down by the beach on a perfect San Diego October day. I saw my wife in her beautiful white dress. Her parents, children, and my parents all gathered as we were married. I remember thinking, *this will always be one of the most memorable days of my life*. And to this day, it still is.

We stayed in a small place in Pacific Beach that night. It was like a fairytale, but I knew through all the joy and relief of coming home, a lot of work was waiting to be done.

That following Monday, I hit the ground running. I checked in with my parole officer, who had me on high control gang supervision right from the gate due to my past affiliations. He was very clear I would more than likely be on parole for three years, despite others who got off in only a year. It was frustrating, but once again, I was up for the challenge.

Next was the DMV, and last but not least my visit at Rise Up Industries. I was told a decision could be made after I had a psychosocial interview. Rise Up offered me help with some resources for temporary work that I highly appreciated. I thought it very interesting that even though they were just considering me for enrollment, they were still very concerned and supportive of my reentry and making sure I knew how to access the things I needed, including recovery meetings, an AA sponsor, Medi-Cal, and other assistance. That really meant a lot to me.

I worked through the holidays doing demolition for a construction company and hoped that Rise Up would accept me. I felt I had to prepare in case it didn't happen. I began to look for long-term work and applied to a few places, like General Dynamics and GM. I had gotten pretty good at welding in prison and earned a few small certifications during the pandemic. I thought this could be a good fit if Rise Up didn't hire me.

During that time, I also had a very strong desire to finish my Bachelor's degree. I'd just completed my third associate's degree right before I was released. I reached out to Project Rebound, a program that helps formerly incarcerated individuals reintegrate and seek higher education at San Diego State University (SDSU).

Soon I had a Project Rebound student worker, along with a Grossmont Community College counselor, helping me through the college application process. "Might as well shoot for the stars," she'd said.

I had thirty days to get all my transcripts, personal statements, recommendation letters, and financial aid filings together. Many nights I'd come home from work and peck away on the Chromebook keyboard, often frustrated and questioning myself. Everything had to be done online, and this was a whole new world for me. My wife was the biggest support through all this – even processes she didn't know how to do, she helped me look up. I honestly don't know where I'd be without her. I finally submitted everything and gave it to the Lord in prayer.

I also focused on the things parole required: my recovery meetings, anger management, and kept going to church as well. I wanted to continue a positive program and keep my circle small at first.

I struggled with being married now, too. For most new marriages, there's a balance that needs to be struck. I was experiencing Post Incarceration Syndrome and anxiety as well. Many things would trigger it.

I talked to Jonathan, Rise Up's deputy director a few days later. When he asked me how I was doing, I told him about everything that was going on. I was feeling overwhelmed having registered for night classes, applying for longer-term work while working another job, navigating the struggles of being a newlywed, and on top of this, I had hydroplaned and crashed my car earlier that week.

He was super supportive and offered any help and guidance I may need. Then he asked me, "Mike, you have a lot of goals, do you feel you can commit to our program for the full eighteen months?"

"Yes," I told him. "I want to." He then shared that they'd like to offer me a position in Rise Up's reentry program to start in January, a few weeks later.

I was so happy. I felt like a weight lifted off my shoulders. I knew I would have help and support in the success I desired and had worked so hard to take hold of. I shared this news with my wife and family, and they were excited and grateful as well.

Within a few weeks I started at Rise Up. I was very grateful and relieved to be investing in my family and my future. College acceptance was still a distant goal, but I needed a practical trade I could use to provide for my family and that would be less physically demanding on my now aging body than the demolition work I had been doing.

I quickly grew to love the program and found the work fascinating. Yet, I was still struggling with finding balance with my wife. We would frequently argue about a variety of conflicting views and circumstances. I started questioning our relationship and whether I misjudged my ability to be a husband. I'd get frustrated and just want to leave. I was angry and at times I did not understand why I was angry at all. I even moved out late one night.

I knew I loved Nicol with all my heart and wanted to be with her, but I felt we differed on vital things. I realized I wasn't good at processing how someone else was feeling. I mean, everything was so new and amazing for me out here, but I was still learning how to be in a relationship like this. The person I loved and cherished was still getting used to me as well. But I wasn't able to hear her, fearing any altercation would lead to us ending.

The night I moved out, I went to sleep at my mom and stepdad's. That following day, early in the Rise Up parking lot, I questioned if I had what it took to successfully be part of this program, handle night classes, and remain married.

I remember praying and realizing in my heart I needed to ask for help. I just wasn't sure how. I kept my head down, watery eyes hidden, and simply tried to stay busy.

That doesn't go far at Rise Up. Darren, a supervisor, noticed and pulled me aside. I shared what I'd been going through. Nicol and I had even started some counseling, but that therapist only made our time together worse, telling us she may not be able to help us.

Darren took me to Dustin, the Rise Up shop supervisor. They closed the door and allowed me to share, cry, and feel sad. They really cared about what I was going through and not the work I felt I needed to get back to. I felt better.

Later that day, after talking amongst themselves, they asked me if my wife and I would be willing to start couples' counseling with their psychologist. "Of course," I said. But I wasn't sure Nicol would, since the last one only made things harder.

I talked to my wife, and she said she would do whatever it would take for us to get through this together. We started couples' counseling, I moved back home with her, and soon I believed in us again!

My wife and I are now going on two years of marriage, and she is, and forever will remain, the love of my life. I'm forever in debt to Rise Up for helping me and Nicol through those overwhelming first few months.

Nicol is grateful for Rise Up and what they've done for us as well. She's always finding things to give and donate to the guys and looks forward to the fundraisers she's held to help the program. This means the world to me.

At Rise Up, I found something I believed in and a place that believed in me as well. I soon began to participate in the speaking engagements they offered and found I enjoy them. It fulfills me to share my experiences and journey of redemption with younger people, offering them the hope that they can avoid these pitfalls and maybe never join a gang or go to prison.

I also finally got my first college acceptance letter from UC Riverside. Then one from UC Irvine, UCLA, SDSU, and last but not least UCSD!

I swayed back and forth between accepting UCSD and SDSU, the two local schools. But with all the help that Project Rebound at SDSU had given me, my mind was set on my being an Aztec.

My mom and stepdad, my wife, in-laws, stepchildren, and grandson were so happy and supportive of my decision.

School began. Fifteen units and a full-time job was so exciting, but boy was I busy. I loved every moment of it. Before long, I was invited to join Project Rebound's staff as a Department of Juvenile Justice mentor. I would engage with the kids in California Youth Authority and San Diego Juvenile Facilities. This was a huge moment in my journey to walk back into a place I'd grown up in, not as a detainee but as a teacher and mentor. Now I teach multiple times a week in the local juvenile halls.

There are many hard days, navigating life's struggles outside of my control, but I no longer allow them to break me down, defeat me, or send me into a spiral of self-destruction. I pray and thank out loud that I have a very amazing support team, both at home and at work.

In July 2023, I graduated from Rise Up and started working for them as a Project Manager. I am also entering my senior year of classes at SDSU on route to earning my Bachelor of Arts in Sociology. I am serving the population I came from in juvenile halls. This all magnifies my ability to have a positive influence and maximize my impact on my San Diego community.

I find true meaning in speaking at so many events and programs, conveying the idea that change is real and possible, inspiring hope and the chance of dreams again, and connecting people to those safe, positive places that will enable them to make their dreams a reality. I love having my parents close by and the ability to communicate with my loved ones regularly. Planning my life with Nicol and deciding how we desire to empower others with our lives and stories of triumph thrills me. These things are my joy and happiness.

Ten, twenty, or thirty years ago, I could not tell you my life would ever look like this. I would not trade my life today for anything.

I'm excited to see how far and long this can go. I cannot regain all those years lost, but God has a way of giving to those who were once without. I thank my Lord Jesus Christ, my family and friends, Rise Up Industries, Project Rebound, and all the others who've empowered me, supported me, and never, ever doubted my ability.

To those still stuck in the chains of addiction, behind the walls of incarceration, and bound by the dysfunction of gang affiliations, freedom is a reality. Look within yourselves, know your worth, and take that first needed step for your journey.

Rewriting the Ink

Frank Perez

Survival Mode

Growing up, I thought I had a pretty good life. I was the middle child. My sister was three years older and my brother was one year younger. I grew up on a ranch with horses, goats, chickens, and rabbits. We played sports and enjoyed going on family outings to amusement parks, visiting relatives, and riding to the mountains to camp in the snow. My mom would take us to Disneyland and to Dodgers games. It was exciting and fun.

However, these good moments were always short-lived. My father was an alcoholic and whenever he would start drinking, which was nearly every day, he would become angry, verbally and physically abusing me, my siblings, and my mom. The violence and anger were so normal that even our pet parrot picked up on it, warning us when my dad was coming home. The parrot would say "Kiko [which is what we called my dad] viene, viene, a correr correr!" "Kiko is coming, run, run!"

Other times, I remember sitting down trying to eat a meal, and my dad would blow up. The tortilla would be cold, and he would start to beat on the table and yell. There was always something he was complaining about. It was scary. It was so hard to eat meals, never knowing when or how he was going to lash out and who would be the target. I developed intestinal issues from the trauma and uncertainty of his behavior that still affect me to this day.

By the time I entered kindergarten, I was so traumatized that I suffered from a speech impediment and was afraid of everything. I stuttered and had to take special speech classes. The kids would pick on me when I would talk.

One day, I came home crying to my father because I was getting picked on by a classmate. My dad slapped me and told me, "Go handle it. I'm not going to have any sissies living under my roof."

I was now afraid. If I didn't find a way to "handle it," I wouldn't have a place to live. My dad would throw me out. I was in survival mode and learning that expressing my emotions would lead to more beatings and verbal abuse at home. I had to keep everything bottled up for self-preservation. I didn't have anyone I could talk to about myself or our family problems.

I realized later in life that growing up I never had the luxury of learning how to properly process any emotions, especially hurt, pain, shame, guilt, and even love. And by this point, I didn't feel I was worthy of support and love. It was easier to resort to anger and violence rather than deal with these emotions. Anger and violence were becoming a major part of who I was. It got me respect and seemed to solve all my problems.

Violence. That's the way I would "handle it." That's how my father would handle situations at home.

The next time that same kid picked on me, I hit him in the face.

He immediately stopped picking on me. I felt a sense of power and control in that moment. I wasn't afraid of anyone at school anymore. Even my stuttering at school lessened as my self-confidence grew.

Or that's what I thought.

Due to all my fighting, I gained respect from the kids in and outside of school. The greater sense of power and recognition I got made me want more. So I kept at it.

However, in sixth grade, there was an incident that made me stop looking for fights the same way. I was in the middle of fighting this boy when his sister jumped on my back, pulling my long hair and yelling "You're going to kill him! He's a hemophiliac! He's going to bleed to death!"

I didn't know what those words meant, but they made something shift in me. I realized I wasn't fighting to hurt him; I was fighting to release myself from all the negative, painful emotions I was feeling.

After that, I stopped picking random fights. I still fought but it was now against people who I believed had it coming, individuals who showed any negativity or aggression toward me or my family and loved ones. It's how I validated violence as my way of life.

A Mother's Bond

I've always been close to my mom. Our bond started when I was really young. She would pick me up early from school and we would go for rides in the car. We would go to the mountains or the beach, sometimes for days at a time. We would go fishing, have picnics, and enjoy each other's company. I learned later that these were times that my father was being violent toward her, and these trips were actually to get away from him. We developed a really strong bond because of this time we shared together – just my mom and me. We were like Bonnie and Clyde.

Those were the good times with her. She wouldn't talk about what happened with my dad, but I knew. There were many nights that I would wake up in the middle of the night, hearing my mom screaming as my dad beat her. We lived like that for years. By the time I was eight years old, I would start getting in the middle of them, running to my mom's aid. I had to protect her. But then my dad would start beating on me.

When I was 15, my older sister died in a car accident. My family had never experienced a tragedy of this magnitude. We didn't know how to properly process her loss. So individually we dealt with her loss the best way we knew how. My father sunk deeper into his alcoholism and debauchery. My mother turned to God, and my brother and I numbed the pain with drugs and violence.

It was at this time that my propensity for violence escalated from physical fights to a level where I really wanted to hurt my adversary. Weapons became the norm – I was really trying to hurt people in a bad way to cope with the pain and stress I was experiencing but didn't know how to process.

The same year that my sister died, my dad swung at me, and I knocked him out. The relationship I had with my pop was never the same after that. I knew I was strong enough to beat him up, so anytime he tried to lay a hand on my mom and I was around, I would protect her. But it took its toll on me. The violence toward my mom still escalated. There was just a lot of madness throughout the house, and it's still hard for me to talk about.

My closeness with my mom and my inability to process my anger in a healthy way led me to take extreme actions. Sometimes, I would come home to my mom on the floor all beaten up, with two black eyes and teeth busted out. I would have to take her to the hospital to get her fixed up.

Then I would wait for my dad to come home. I would just sit on the porch, sharpening up my knife. My brother would stop him in the driveway and tell him to get out of here. He would leave, and stay away for several days at a time, but two or three weeks later, he would work his way back into the house.

My mom would ask me not to hurt him, that she would fix it. By then, my rage would have subsided enough that I believed her. I truly wanted to believe that she would fix it. So we let him come back into the house each time.

But the cycle would start again.

I was conflicted. I wanted to protect my mom but the only way I knew how to do that was to physically hurt my dad, and my mom wouldn't let me do that. I didn't want to hurt my mom more than she already was, so I would verbally tell my dad, "If you ever, ever put your hands on my mom again, I'm going to kill you." But even when he said he wouldn't hurt her, within a few months, he would do it again. It was relentless.

When I was seventeen, I realized this cycle wasn't going to change and I needed to get away. I moved out of the house to live on my own. Things were going a little better for me – until my eighteenth birthday. I came home to check on my mom to find her fighting with my father's girlfriend, rolling around in the parking lot outside our home. My dad was just sitting there watching.

I had a deep sinking feeling that my mom was going to die this way. If I didn't stand up for her honor, no one else would. I wanted nothing more than to put an end to all of this for her. I looked at my father and said to him, "You're dead."

But instead, I killed his twenty-two-year-old, drug addict girlfriend a couple days later. I let my dad live so he could live with the pain that my mom and I felt every time he would beat on us. That was my justification.

When I was 18 years old, my thinking was so far out of line from social norms that, in my mind, taking a life was justifiable. But it's never justifiable.

A short time later, I was arrested and charged with premeditated first-degree murder with special allegations. The District Attorney sought the death penalty. Eventually I was sentenced to 25 years to life and, full of hate and rage, I was sent to the California Department of Corrections to start my life sentence. Prison became my "home" for the next 38 years.

Prison: Life Continued

For years I felt helpless and hopeless. California Governor Gray Davis said that the only way a Lifer was going to get out of prison was in a pine box.

I spent those first several years learning how I was going to live the rest of my life in prison. To protect myself, I felt I had to go deeper into the violence I was already so familiar with. From the beginning, I fell into the regular life of the gang – a lot of violence, a lot of drugs. I worked hard, and I was a good fighter. Whenever riots would kick off, I would push up to the front. The other side would always send me the big guys and I would fight them. And I'd win.

Yet, I also had a thirst for knowledge. I focused on my education, and over the years, I got my high school diploma. I became a bilingual teacher's aide and helped English language learners improve their speaking skills. In 1999, thirteen years after entering prison, I was transferred to Ironwood State Prison where I had the opportunity to go to college under an Equal Opportunity program (EOPS) to earn my AS in Business Management.

Every time I moved to a new prison, I had to learn what programs the prison had to offer and how to fit into the yard politics. I engaged in the violence for years, even while I focused on my education. I felt like I was living a double life.

My brother was my cellie twice – once in 2004 for a couple months until he paroled and then again in 2006. I had influence on the yard during those times, so when my brother was put in my building, I would force out my other cellie and move my brother in. We were close growing up, always looking out for each other. By 2004, we hadn't seen each other for 17 years, so it was nice having him nearby again.

When he paroled the second time, he died of an overdose six days later. His death was another tragedy – my sister's death and life in prison being two others – that rocked me to the core.

After he died, I got deeper into the violence and the drugs. I wanted to see how deep I could go and then see if I could get out of it. I would go to ad seg (solitary confinement) to clean up, but I would still end up getting more drugs in there. It was a roller coaster ride. But something was starting to shift in me.

Spending much of those next five years, from 2006 to 2011, in the SHU for my disruptive behavior, I had time to reflect. I started thinking differently about life and about my brother. I knew I needed to make some changes in my life if I didn't want to die in prison.

It was in those years that, slowly, I made a personal commitment to myself to make changes in my life. It didn't happen overnight, but with the seeds of change planted in my brain, my thoughts began to change from thinking like a criminal to thinking about how to make myself a better person. It wasn't a straightforward process. I first went deeper into the gang culture and violence before I was able to draw myself out of it again.

My real shift started in 2012 when I officially dropped out of the gang. I was taking cognitive behavioral therapy (CBT) classes and attending Criminals and Gang Members Anonymous (CGA), Narcotics Anonymous (NA), and self-help groups. I started learning about the ripple effect. In my mind, I had never hurt or caused harm to anyone who didn't deserve it. But now I was learning about the impacts of my actions on my victims' families. I realized that I had created a lot of victims in my life. Even if I had thought my primary victim had it coming, their families and loved ones did not. I started making direct amends and living amends by changing the way I lived my life – no more gangs, no more violence.

And then there was what my mom said to me.

Many of the decisions I made in prison were made with my mother in mind. My mom would come visit me, support me, and we would talk on the phone regularly.

One time, she came to visit and told me, "I'm by myself. Everyone is dead. I need you home."

"They're never going to let me out, Mom. You have to understand that. They're never going to let me out," I responded.

But she kept on me like that. "I need you home."

Two years later, she came back and a light bulb went off for me. "Look," she said, "you put in 31 years for the homies. It's time you put in some work for me."

That set me permanently on my trajectory to change.

Although it still took me eight additional years to get out, I knew at this point that I needed to gain more insight into the motivations for my past actions.

CBT wasn't working for me so I started looking for something else. That's when I stumbled upon Rational Emotive Behavior Therapy (REBT). With REBT, I was able to stay more consistently on the path of change. I got a psychologist, Roy F., in 2018 who worked with me to think rationally. He helped me realize all the little things that triggered me and how I could think my way out of those negative situations. Change didn't happen as fast as I would have liked, but eventually change did happen.

There were, of course, setbacks along the way. I had made real changes in my life, but when I went to the parole board, they gave me the worst denial of my life. I got a five-year denial when I had previously been getting two- or three-year denials. It made me shut down for a period. Screw everything. I went back to my old ways. But something didn't feel right. I didn't like how my old ways felt anymore.

The next time I went to the Board, I went in with the mentality that they were not going to let me out of prison. I still wanted to build a good case for myself. They had previously said I lacked remorse and insight, so I made sure I was able to present them with the ABC model this time – how the events in my life caused me to have certain feelings and thoughts, which then lead to my actions, and ultimately my crime.

This opened the doors. The commissioner saw my sincerity. I could now empathize with my victims and see my crime through their eyes. I had made a real change and was found suitable for parole.

A New Life Sentence

Despite being found suitable for parole, it wasn't a guarantee that I would be released from prison. When the Board finds someone suitable, they have 120 days to finalize that decision, so I was waiting 120 days to see if it would hold. Then the governor has thirty days after that to approve or decline the suitability. In my mind, they were going to pull my date. I had been found unsuitable for parole eleven times before.

But 120 days went by, and the Board didn't pull my date. Thirty more days, and the governor didn't pull it either.

I was in a state of disbelief throughout the 150 days between being found suitable and the expected date of my release. Those were the most stressful 150 days of my life. But before I knew it, the day came. I walked through the prison doors. I was out.

The challenges started immediately. My deceased brother's girlfriend, who I still consider my sister picked me up from the gate the day I got out. Some friendships last for life – ours is one of them.

We stopped at a Starbucks because she had to use the bathroom; I did, too. When we went in, she walked straight to the restroom. It wasn't that easy for me. I saw symbols by the door that I hadn't seen before. There was a girl and a boy on the same sign, so I thought I couldn't go in that room. The other door had the same symbols.

When another woman walked into the second bathroom, I thought, *Phew, I'm glad I didn't go in there.* But I didn't know where I could go. My sister had to explain to me that the symbols meant anybody could use the restroom.

Finally relieved, I then couldn't even figure out how to turn on the water to wash my hands. The automatic faucets and soap dispensers confused me. *When did going to the bathroom get so difficult?*

Everything felt like a challenge. I had just finished doing 38 years in prison and would live for the first six months in a halfway house with four other men. I quickly had to learn how to manage my own life and reprogram myself by establishing a socially acceptable routine: to wake up at a certain time, get to work on time, work eight hours a day, buy groceries, and make my own meals. I didn't have to think about these things in prison. Now, adjusting to civil life was either sink or swim – and drowning was not an option.

Things that should have been easy were not. I didn't know how to get on the bus. I didn't know how to ride the trolley. I had no idea how to use a cell phone or pay my bills. I had no documents – no birth certificate, no ID, no social security card, no driver's license, nothing. And everywhere I went with a State ID, nobody wanted to honor it.

I spent my first month out hunting down my documents. In the beginning, I had no help, and I was getting nowhere, just more frustrated. Then, a girl who was also in the halfway house took me under her wing and showed me the ropes.

She taught me how to use the bus and trolley, but still I was getting nowhere. Everywhere I went, I needed one ID to get another one. I felt like I wasted a month going back and forth.

Finally, my nephew was able to go on the internet and get my birth certificate. With that, I was able to get everything else. Things started changing for the better.

One of my friends from prison told me about the Center for Employment Opportunities (CEO), an organization that helps individuals who have just gotten out of prison or jail with job training. He had paroled a few years earlier and was now a supervisor there. Right away, I went to CEO, and they hired me to pick up trash on the freeways. It felt like my new life was beginning.

During the three-day orientation at CEO, an incredible thing happened. I met someone. Her name is Dulce. Dulce was in the federal halfway house in San Diego, and I was in a state halfway house in El Cajon. It just so happened that she caught the trolley going one way, I caught the trolley going the other way, and we had the same destination – the Center for Employment Opportunities.

On Day One, I was asked to share with the group about myself. When I shared that I had just gotten out of prison after serving 38 years, she turned around and said, "Welcome home, mijo." I knew right then that she was special, that she was going to be my wife.

We would work together for the next couple months on the highways, picking up trash. It was a humble beginning, but it keeps growing. She has been a major influence in my life already. Most of my family is dead, I don't have any kids, and I thought I would go through life single.

With Dulce in my life, I have a family again – a partner, kids, grandkids, uncles, aunts, and more. I've been able to help her rekindle her relationship with her children. The biggest difference to me is that I now have a responsibility to a family that I love. It's helping me stay focused and on track. Dulce and I both have had a tough past with criminal histories and prior drug addictions, but we were both able to overcome that, and now we're just trying to make a home for ourselves, together.

One day, after I had been working at CEO for about a month, my parole officer showed up at my door and said, "Hey Perez, I have a job for you."

"I already have a job," I responded. I was still working at CEO and doing well.

"This is a better job for you." She went on to tell me about Rise Up Industries' Computer Numerical Control (CNC) machinist apprenticeship program. At the time, she didn't tell me it was a reentry program, but since she was strongly encouraging me, I figured I would go check it out and see what it was all about. I felt the push from her that I needed to go get this job.

After a tour and a conversation with the staff at Rise Up, I really liked what was being offered. It was a career, not just a job. At the end of the 18-month apprenticeship, I would earn a certificate to be a

CNC Machine Operator. It's a job that pays well and does not require a lot of manual labor. It's the type of work I can do all the way into my 80s. When Rise Up offered me the job, I accepted.

Rise Up offered everything I felt I needed to succeed, starting with a support network including mentors, psychologists, counselors, case managers, math teachers, and supervisors. It is more than just work. They teach life skills - some of which I didn't know I needed: how to budget, pay my bills, make appointments online, handle insurance, make shopping lists, communicate effectively, everything. They have also been supportive in helping me learn how to socialize and interact with people within the boundaries of societal norms. I've had to work to overcome my institutionalization. I know it's going to be a lifetime of learning.

Still, even with a great support network, things haven't been easy. The biggest ongoing hurdle for me is technology – cell phones and computers. Everything is done online today. When I was sent to prison, cell phones, laptops, and computers were basically non-existent. I missed out on the whole technological era.

Coming out almost four decades later, the whole world is being run by computers. Even when I use the phone to call a doctor's office, it's all automated.

The first time I made a phone call and there was an automated menu, I was dumbfounded. I honestly didn't understand what was going on and almost hung up. I just wanted to speak to a human being. I don't think I'll ever learn all of it, but I'm learning enough to get around on a daily basis and I'm grateful for my progress.

I feel like I'm 40 years behind. I'm playing catch up, including with my savings, my 401k. I may only have 20 years of working left, if I'm lucky. But I really don't want to be working into my 80s. What's helping me is knowing that I have responsibilities to my family. That gives me motivation to keep moving forward. I want to feel secure financially, so I can live the life I want to live. I'm going to keep getting older, I'm going to get sick, and the reality is money makes the world go round.

I went into prison when I was young. I want today's youth to find better ways than I could. If there are problems going on at home, don't hold it in. Talk about it to someone. One thing I've learned for sure is that eventually, what is held in is going to come out. It's going to explode one way or another. I want today's youth to know that just because this happened or that happened, life isn't over. It's a hurdle that you have to learn to get over. Don't ever think that you're hopeless or helpless because there is help. You just have to ask for it.

I keep trying and pushing forward because I'd rather be out here than in there. There's a lot I have to learn. I'm optimistic about the future that I'll be able to do it. Life is going to keep giving me obstacles and challenges. Learning what I'm learning here at Rise Up, I know it's going to help me a lot. There will be challenges that I don't yet know how to overcome, but one way or another, I will figure it out.

Rewriting the Ink

Rewriting the Ink

Rewriting the Ink

Jesse Avina

A Message to a Child

My childhood was that of a typical child from a Mexican household. I would often get woken up to loud Mexican music and my mother singing along. There were always people around, especially on the weekends – my parents, my brother, my cousins, and my grandma. We would all eat meals together at the table. I'd have to do chores, too, especially cleaning, all around the house. My brother, mom, and I would often go to church on Sundays.

I was fortunate to have both parents in my life at this very critical time. Most of the kids that I went to school with had both their parents too, so I figured this was the only way to be seen as normal.

My brother and I were about four years apart in age. We didn't have a lot in common, but we always got along. I would tease him whenever I beat him at a game we were playing. We leaned on each other to feel some type of comfort in our home.

My mother always showed the best type of real care and concern for me and my brother. She was a stay-at-home mom who made sure the food was made when we got home from school and that we had everything we needed. She was constantly showing affection by giving us hugs and kisses and taking pictures to document all of our memories.

My father had always been really strict but had never misled my brother or me. Everything that he taught us made sense and always had a strong purpose. My father taught my brother and me a lot about soccer, like offensive and defensive techniques. He taught us how to be competitive and to always do our best. He also taught us about keeping our word at all times. If we said we were going to do something, we better make sure we followed through with it. He instilled in my brother and me to always be hard workers no matter what the task was – what we did reflected back to our last name, so we should always keep that in mind.

From my father I was also taught never to hit women and to respect them no matter what. He made it a point to instill that in my head over and over again since I was very young. So when I saw my father hit my mother for the first time, my feelings, emotions, and everything inside of me was confused. I was so confused because I based a big part of my life on what I was taught by my father. He had been the one to show me right and wrong, so now I didn't know what to believe. He had lied to me in the biggest way.

After that, he and my mother separated. Then came the most difficult part of my childhood: being a child with divorced parents. My brother and I went to live with our mother. I had based so much of my identity off of having two parents, as that was normal in my eyes from all the families I would see at school.

To make the situation worse, my brother and I would always be put in the middle of their arguments. It was so stressful when they would make us pick sides. Having to deal with that stress at such a young age made me question what were the right or wrong feelings and emotions. I didn't know if it was okay to start feeling resentment toward my father, I didn't know if having negative emotions would get me in trouble, and I didn't know if I was in the wrong for feeling confused for not knowing what to believe was right.

It was the worst around the holidays. Since they were now separated, me and my brother would be asked where we wanted to celebrate that holiday and have to pick sides. If I chose to go with my mother, my father would speak bad about her, and he would try to make me believe that I didn't love and care for him. If I chose to go with my father, my mother would say that I didn't love her and that if my father really loved me and my brother, then he wouldn't have broken up our family. No matter what we chose, my brother and I were never able to make our parents happy or make the right choice. I knew even at that young age that our parents making us choose between them was inappropriate.

My brother and I still loved our parents. Having to choose between them was hard because we didn't want to hurt anyone's feelings. They wanted to know who we loved most, even though we loved them equally. I knew my brother and I were never going to be split up – one going with our mom and one going with our dad. We would stick it out together and lean on each other for comfort.

Even though I knew it was not right to hit women, I still loved and cared for my father. But something had changed. It was as if I had developed hate for him as well. From that day forward, I felt like I didn't need him around me and my little brother in the same way. I had to venture out and see things for myself. I couldn't believe anything else he said. His lying to me was an ultimatum for me to stand on my own two feet.

Finding a Home on the Streets

After my mother and father separated, my mother had to work to provide for us, so she got a full-time job. I never really knew what she did, but knowing that she was working to provide for me and my brother gave me more respect for her. However, her working all the time meant she was hardly ever home. My mother had hired a babysitter to watch over us while she was at work, but knowing that our babysitter couldn't punish me in any way worked in my favor. I knew I could get away with more.

I took to the streets. Being in the streets helped me see that the majority of my friends had dysfunctional families, too – many had absent fathers and some had never met their fathers at all. Having that void in our lives made all of us turn to each other for any kind of guidance. Being in the streets gave me a sense of comfort and belonging. I knew that I could be in trouble at home, but as soon as my mom went to work, the streets were always there to welcome me with open arms. I would feel adrenaline and excitement when I was with my friends in the streets.

The more I was in the streets and away from rules, the more I continued to do whatever I wanted. The sense of comfort and excitement that I felt with my friends in the street was new to me. For the first time, I felt welcomed.

Everyone had a reason why they chose to be in the streets. Some of my friends had parents that were absent so they had no authority figures at home. Some had older brothers and sisters that were in the justice system for making bad choices. Some had parents that didn't care enough about them to worry about what they did. In a way, I was relieved knowing that other friends had the same struggles at home. I didn't feel so embarrassed or different anymore.

My friends and I would commit small crimes in the beginning. The crimes became more serious as time went by and we all came to know that we were going to have each other's backs and not tell on each other. We would tag just about anything – walls, trucks, freeways, whatever would catch someone's attention – but mainly in our enemies' neighborhood. By tagging in our enemies' area, we wanted to create more conflict and drama.

Beer runs were another small crime that we would do almost daily because we were all too young to buy alcohol. At the time, alcohol wasn't something that caught my interest enough to where I would do any and everything to have it. Some of my friends would drink with the expectation to get drunk, but the rest of us preferred different ways, like drugs, to end the day.

What excited me the most was the fighting. Fights were the biggest reason that I wanted to be in the streets and in my neighborhood. Sometimes my friends and I fought amongst ourselves, and other times we would fight against our rivals, crosstowns, or just anyone who disliked our neighborhood. We viewed fighting as one of the ways we could show our drive and just how much dedication we had to our neighborhood.

I remember when things started getting more serious. The change from small crimes to more serious crimes started when my friends and I physically hurt someone while committing a beer run at a liquor store. A man attempted to physically stop us in the act, but my friends and I were not going to allow anyone to interfere with us having a good time. At that moment, in my mind, any physical altercation seemed harmless. I thought fighting was just a way to prove a point.

Everything had been going as usual. Then, from one second to the next, everything started going real slow, and next thing I knew, a fist fight involving the owner and this bystander started. I realized that two of my friends were involved, and so there was no alternative but to join in. Next thing I knew, I was fighting to get the owner off of my friend. We wanted to get away to not escalate the situation anymore, but the owner and bystander kept coming at us, so we were forced to stand our ground.

The more we tried to get away, the more serious the crime became. Now it had turned into a robbery, GBI (great bodily injury), assault with a weapon, and other charges I can't remember. That sudden change in how serious the crime had become was a big eye opener on how our actions could become more serious than intended.

This incident was a turning point. In the back of my mind, I knew I shouldn't be rolling the dice with something so serious, but I still had so much excitement and anticipation to see what could happen if I chose to go all in this game. My self-pride and self-respect didn't allow me to back out or go against our bond and street code. I didn't want to jeopardize losing the feeling of belonging if I chose to leave the streets. So I made a commitment to myself and to my friends that I would follow through with this new way of life.

The Beginning of Two Different Worlds

I remember going to Juvenile Hall for the first time when I was thirteen, and, for some weird and wrong reason, I felt excited instead of nervous. Since I already knew the way my lifestyle was heading, I was expecting this to happen eventually. The ride to Juvenile Hall was long and uncomfortable. I was cuffed for the first time. I kept thinking about wanting to get through this so I could get back out to the streets. I felt adrenaline thinking about the fights I heard friends talk about and had a sense of excited anticipation to participate in the fighting myself. I remember wondering how much time I was going to have to do for the minor charges I had before I could get back out to the streets.

At the same time, I kept thinking about what my mom was going to say or how she was going to react when she came to see me in person. I knew she was going to be mad and disappointed. I had let her down. I never wanted her to feel like me making bad choices was her fault. She had always taught me right from wrong; she knew I knew better than to get caught up in this.

The Juvenile Hall smelled like feet, and it was cold like a hospital. The food was nasty, and the clothes were old and worn out. Putting on the worn-out clothes gave me the feeling of being helpless.

While being there, I had to learn how to make the best of my situation. The seven months I spent in Juvenile Hall that first time were a waste. There was nothing to do. Still, from one day to another, time flew by since I didn't have to think about anything important.

I was in and out of Juvenile Hall for the next couple of years before being put in a program called Drug Court that was really strict and made it really difficult to do what I wanted. They wanted to give me more structure and instill more fear of the system in me. This program used incarceration as a way to force rehabilitation. I remember thinking that it might not have been the best way to help me learn from my bad choices, but it did have a positive effect in the long run.

They made me go to groups multiple days a week, go to school, and check in regularly with the officers. There were so many stipulations I had to follow. I was getting tested for drugs every day. When I gave a positive urine analysis, I would be taken back to Juvenile Hall for the weekend. The consistency of being locked up over the weekend for the smallest infraction made me want to hurry up, comply with their demands, and finish my term so I could be left alone and able to do as I pleased.

By the time I turned 19, I had been out of trouble for almost two years. During those two years, I got to experience being a father. Immediately after my daughter was born, I knew that I wanted to be there for her and would do whatever it took to stay out of trouble. I had had my first son two years earlier while I was in Drug Court, but I was not fortunate to experience being a parent for him. I wanted to do it differently this time.

With my daughter, I learned that there is nothing else like being a father. Being depended on and having to provide for someone other than just myself was new to me, but ensuring I made it happen gave me something to look forward to. I got to experience all the hard work parents must do. I had to provide for my daughter and her mother by working a full-time job. I was able to see all the patience and effort that is needed to raise a child and the devotion a parent must give in order for a family to move forward in a healthy and positive manner.

I didn't want to make the same mistakes my father did. I didn't want my daughter to go through the same things I went through. I wanted to be present for her in a way that I couldn't be for my son and that my father wasn't for me. I didn't want to lay a hand on a woman either, so I worked hard to be a good father and a good partner.

I watched my daughter take her first steps, attempt to say her first words, and I enjoyed all the happiness a child can bring. I can honestly say that I was fortunate to experience the rewards of being a parent. I will never forget seeing the expressions of excitement on my daughter's face when I would teach her something new, like walking on the inside of the sidewalk for her safety or holding my hand when crossing the street.

When my daughter was nearly two years old, her mother and I realized we were not compatible partners. We had very different goals for our lives at that time and were not able to find a common ground that was fit for any child to be around. I knew it was best for us to separate, but I was distraught because separating took away all the happiness and joy I had found in being around my daughter.

With this privilege no longer being an option, I put my priorities and what was important to me on hold. I did not know how to deal with a loss like this, so I tried to mask out what I was feeling by returning to the lifestyle of the streets and the street code. I stopped taking care of my responsibilities or thinking about the consequences. I became selfish and immature, thinking only about myself and not caring about what was actually important – building a foundation or structure for my life to keep me out of trouble, being a fit parent, and being a good role model for my loved ones – anymore.

Leaving My Comfort Zone

I went to jail for the first time as an adult when I was 19.

After this first time I went to jail, the next seven years flew right by as I was constantly in and out of jail. I spent so much time incarcerated during this time that I made jail my comfort zone. I was able to adapt to the jailhouse code real quick and continue living a similar lifestyle to the streets. I stopped worrying about the amount of time that they would give me each time I was arrested. At the time, I was not realizing how valuable time was in the long run.

When I was 25, almost 26 years old, I began to ask myself why I was not allowing myself to succeed. I knew that I had not reached my full potential. I knew my worth and that I was settling for less. I knew a lot of people cared for me, genuinely cared for me. They would comment that I could do better, that I was wasting my life and talent by being in jail. I looked at the older gentlemen in jail, and I realized I didn't want to be in the same situation – old and locked up.

However, since I had made jail my comfort zone, I was content being there and in that situation. But I was really just being selfish and in denial. I kept coming up with excuses about why I would keep going back to jail. It didn't feel like a possibility for me to stop the cycle and get out of the habit. I never thought that my being in jail was hurting anyone. My mom would tell me in Spanish that I wasn't the only one locked up. I didn't understand what she meant by that.

But when I started to think about the people I cared for, I realized that it hurt me to watch them suffer or see them going through hardship. I realized the same was true for them about me, too. My mom cared and wanted the best for me; my decisions were hurting her.

One time, my mother came to visit me in jail and told me my grandma was sick. She came again the next week and shared that my grandma was not getting any better. That's when it hit me that I may not see my grandma again. I was shocked because I had never pictured her getting sick. I never thought it would happen to her or be that quick.

Growing up, I would see my grandma every weekend. She would come visit us from Mexico. I was her first grandson and, in her eyes, I could do nothing wrong. I could be in trouble with my mom, but my grandma would bypass it and make me feel loved and cared for. She wasn't judgmental. We were really close.

Now, my grandma was on her deathbed, and I was stuck in jail.

Luckily, my mom was able to schedule a sentence modification appointment in court for me to be considered for early release based on the conditions that my grandma was dying. Two weeks later, the court proceedings went through, and I was able to get out a few weeks before I was originally scheduled to be released.

I went straight to the hospital and got to see my grandma before she passed. I was grateful that I got to see her. At the same time, I felt bad because before that day, she was always asking me to stop going back to jail. I was disappointed in myself because I wasn't able to live up to her wishes. I felt like I had let her down.

Although that wasn't my last time in jail, it started the ball rolling where I realized that maybe this jail path wasn't the path I wanted to live anymore.

I went to jail three more times over the next seven years with high hopes that each time would be my last. During the last stint in jail, my dad's mom got sick with COVID-19 and passed away at home. Ten days later, my dad, having just gotten out of quarantine from catching COVID himself, had a diabetic shock and died. Even though we didn't get along for a lot of my life, it was still overwhelming and upsetting to realize that I no longer had a dad. Despite our differences, I know he wanted to see me succeed, and that meant a lot to me.

I struggled with the fact that I felt so comfortable in jail. Even though I didn't want to go back inside and wanted to spend more time outside with my family and work on myself, I was still drawn back in because it was familiar. I was able to maneuver around the environment with ease. I felt capable in there; I had mastered the mentality needed to be incarcerated.

But I've come to realize that sometimes, not knowing what's going to happen in the end is not so much a bad thing. It can be really good. I realize how quickly life can be taken – going to jail or dying. Not trying to predict what will happen tomorrow has helped me enjoy each day as it is. I want to make the most of each day I have, whether I am in jail or out in society. I know I want to be more present and work toward something new and positive for myself. And I don't want to be absent from any more memories that I could be creating together with my family and loved ones.

Trying Something New

By 2022, I was trying something different. I started working at the Center for Employment Opportunities. Four days a week, I was picking up trash on the highways. One day a week, I was working with a counselor to improve my resume and apply for other jobs. That's where I learned about Rise Up Industries.

I applied and had to wait. It was discouraging but I thought it could be worth it, so I stuck it out. Finally, they called me for an interview, and ultimately offered me a start date. I wasn't sure I could make it through the 18-month program or if it was a good fit for me.

I was close-minded. I wasn't open to differences in other people that I wasn't already used to. Giving Rise Up a chance helped me see things in a different way. For myself and for a lot of people that come from the same type of lifestyle, we've never had a positive role model or been in a supportive environment. We don't realize that things can be different. We just roll with what we got. Whatever cards are dealt to us, we think that's just the way it is and that things won't get better.

But at Rise Up, when I started opening myself to the possibility of change, I began to see that things could get better if I wanted them to.

Before even getting hired, one of the members, Mike, called to talk about what Rise Up had to offer. He wanted to put me at ease and help me be more receptive to Rise Up and its stipulations. I was hesitant about the required therapy sessions he mentioned, and what they would consist of. I didn't know if I would be scolded or interrogated. I had never done something like therapy before.

I was also worried about all of the daily structure that Rise Up required. Everything sounded overwhelming and stressful. Even the level of care they pushed on a participant seemed too much. It almost felt like they were painting a perfect picture of their reentry program, but nothing had been perfect in my life. It was too much. I wasn't convinced, but hearing Mike's points about Rise Up's potential benefits made it easier to give Rise Up a shot.

I had nothing to lose. I needed to find a way to get out of my comfort zone and stay out of jail. Being able to physically see how much of a benefit this place was to the other participants helped me mentally want the same for myself. I wanted to experience what it was like to be normal. I wanted to feel the same type of happiness that they felt. I wanted to have a purpose, to do something other than sit in a cell. I wanted to attempt to reach my full potential. I didn't want to just be part of the statistics.

I decided to give it a chance, even though it meant leaving my work at the shipyard and taking a pay cut. I wanted a less backbreaking career, something more mental than physical. Knowing that it wouldn't be so hard on my own body further pushed me to get a career with Rise Up in their machine shop.

I didn't know it at the time, but machining can be useful in a lot of different areas of everyday life, too. It has made me more detail-oriented and given me a different outlook on things that are used every day. Since I started working here, whenever I pick up a tool or something metal, the first thing I think about is if it was made in a machine shop. I wonder if I could make this, or even make it somewhat better. Seeing how something is made and being able to make it myself gives me a better feeling than anything right now.

Mike continued to support me when I started working at Rise Up. He and another member, Komisi, have been my two main positive role models. Since my first day, they made the atmosphere easier to adapt to. They were positive and welcoming, offering real guidance and humble words of advice. Without them, I would still be close-minded and argumentative.

Seeing them and hearing about the changes they've made in their lives gives me a sense of hope and the ability to see things in a new way. I am shocked at how much effort they put into trying to make me feel comfortable here and to show me that things can get better. They came from similar upbringings as me and now have really turned their lives around, even with the obstacles they've had to surpass. This is motivating me to believe that if they can do it, I can do it, too.

They show genuine care and concern for me. Many times as we were leaving for the day, they said, "Hit me up if you need anything." I knew that if I ever needed help, I could call them, and it would be positive. Although I never did, knowing that I had them to count on was a good feeling.

I can count my true friends with one hand. It's hard to come by people who actually want to do right and give a helping hand without wanting anything in return. If I called my homeboys, they would probably get me high in the process of trying to help me. Being around my peers in the streets, no one was doing anything positive, no one was trying to change. Being around them is a revolving door back to jail or prison. Mike and Komisi helped me because they wanted to help me succeed and find a better way.

For example, I used to drive without a license. Komisi would stay on me telling me to go get a license, that it wasn't worth the risk to drive without one. Over and over he told me. I knew I needed to be legit. Around the same time, another member told me about a part-time job he had driving trucks to deliver home appliances to houses. The possibility of more work further encouraged me to apply for my license. So I went to the DMV and got my license.

Rise Up is understanding. If I have to meet probation or have a medical appointment, they are willing to work with me so I meet those requirements. This flexibility within their structure helps me adjust to society and be successful while still having a job. Their patience and concern for every member's wellbeing helps all of us in the long run when we finish the program because we see more possibilities for ourselves and our future.

My time at Rise Up so far has taught me to be a little more open to something new and to stop thinking that there's no other way than the way I know. There's no need to settle for less. I want to keep trying to change and better the cards that were dealt to me. Working here has given me different options that I didn't have before. Now I know how to hold a job, how to be a better employee, and how to be a better human. All of this is because I allowed myself to try something new.

Rewriting the Ink

Rewriting the Ink

Rewriting the Ink

Joseph Scheinuck

Introduction

This story has been difficult to write. Vulnerability does not come easy to me, and I have a hard time each time I share my life story. I have realized, however, that my story does not belong to me. It belongs to all of the people I have hurt; it belongs to the man I murdered, and to his family. It belongs to all of the people who have secrets that keep them on a merry-go-round of shame, anger, rage, and despair.

My story is not really profound – it is actually pretty simple. When we keep painful secrets locked up inside our hearts and minds, we enter onto a path of destruction. Sexual abuse causes severe trauma that, if not dealt with, will become a monster that destroys the lives of its victims and possibly the lives of those around them. Not everyone will respond in the way that I did, but at least some will.

I share my story in the hope that it will reach some of those who have been unable to deal with trauma in a healthy manner. I want to make clear that I in no way blame my actions on the abuse I suffered. I am responsible for how I reacted to what happened to me. I could have chosen to react differently. I wish that I would have asked for help. Shame and guilt can only thrive in a dark place; the light of exposure takes their power away.

An Old Boy

How did a boy become an old man in a day?
Oh... I remember...
I wish that I did not.

I don't remember my father. My parents divorced when I was two years old. I was constantly told by my mother that it was not a pleasant separation: my father was a drunk, cheated on her, and repeatedly tried to kill us by "fixing" the brakes on the car.

When I was six, my father called and asked to see me. My mother stood over me and asked if I wanted to – the tone of her voice and her body language clearly communicating what the answer should be. I didn't meet him.

I don't remember much about these early years. I have faint memories of living with my mom next door to my grandmother's house in a small cottage. Then I remember my mom marrying my stepdad and going to live at his house. Shortly after that, my stepdad adopted me, and my last name changed to Scheinuck.

I did not like having my stepdad around. I felt like he was stealing my mom from me. I was mean to him and can remember purposely starting fights between them. It wasn't the most ideal household for a young boy to live in, especially once I started acting out and getting in trouble a lot.

When I was about seven, my grandmother gave me some money to go to the store for her. I loved going to the Milk Depot. It had a rubber hose across the driveway that would go "ding ding" whenever a car would drive across it, bringing a cashier to the car to see what the customer wanted. The store also had a walk-up service which gave me the opportunity to execute my first theft.

I can't remember what my grandmother had sent me there for, but I came back with a creamsicle ice cream pop that I had grabbed from the counter. She had not given me enough money to buy one, and she asked me how I had gotten it. I hemmed and hawed and finally admitted that I had stolen it. I got a quick spanking, and she told my mother and stepdad what I had done. Boy was I in trouble! I got another whipping and was grounded for what seemed like years.

That didn't stop me. I began to steal more. I stole from my grandma's purse, my aunt Big Aggie's purse, my mother's purse, and from people who would come to our house for events and dinners. I also began stealing from other stores and places. Stealing was easy, exciting, and enjoyable. It was a quick way to get what I wanted.

Something else I found enjoyable as a kid was our yearly family camping trips. My grandpa's brother, Uncle Tony, had been taking the family for over twenty years. It began with my mom and all of her brothers and sisters; she had eight of them! My cousins and I would usually go during the week with Uncle Tony and the adults who had jobs would come on the weekend.

Our camping spot was in a small valley next to a clear mountain stream full of small trout that we would eagerly catch and cook in butter wrapped with tin foil. We would go hiking downstream to different pools and waterfalls where we would swim, fish, and climb rocks. Barefoot all day, staying up till late in the night listening to ghost stories around the campfire – it was a blast.

I looked forward to these trips; they were the highlight of my young years. That is, until they were ruined by my cousin, Mark. Mark was one of my older cousins who was always in trouble for something or other. On one trip when I was about nine years old, I cussed or said something that a boy my age should not say. Mark told me that I had to do something for him or he would tell on me. He then proceeded to open up the fly of his zipper and pulled himself out. He forced me to...

It was brief, but horrifying. I felt disgusted and quickly found a way to make it end. He threatened me and told me not to say anything to anyone.

Something broke in me that day. An innocence that I didn't even know I had was stolen. I did not know it at the time, but that was the first in a series of events that would lead me down a path of destruction and misery. It would ruin not only my life but the lives of many others, including the man I murdered in 1993 and the family who is still grieving his loss today, thirty years after his death.

There were other incidents of sexual abuse. Some I remember quite clearly, others not so well. I began to feel like I could not trust anyone, even my family. At the time, I wouldn't have stated it that way, but looking back I can see it clearly. I began to isolate, rebel, and act out in various ways. I didn't really have a safe place to deal with the trauma, and even if

I did have a safe place, I probably wouldn't have thought to say anything.

I was never told what sexual abuse was. I just knew that what was happening to me felt "bad" and "good" at the same time. It was confusing and I was not equipped to deal with it, so I dug deeper into the stealing that I had already started doing to give me a feeling of at least some control in my life.

My home life was tumultuous. My parents were not the best at dealing with a rebellious child. They did what they could under the circumstances, but there was a lot of frustration that I interpreted as them not wanting me around. At school, I was constantly acting out, being suspended, getting detention, and giving my teachers the blues. Part of the problem was undiagnosed ADHD, but I think my acting out was due mostly to the effects of the sexual abuse and the unprocessed trauma associated with it.

Around the age of eleven, I began to run away. I would stay gone for days, sleeping in parked cars, in tree forts, behind stores – anywhere I could roll out one of the blankets I had taken from home. I ran away so many times that soon there were no more blankets in the house! I felt more at home in the streets than I did in the house. I always felt like I was just tolerated in my house, like I was in the way and that my parents would be happier to not have to deal with me.

As time went on, I started to use drugs. Stealing was my go-to crime to fuel my new habit. I eventually began doing burglaries of small businesses and fruit stands in the area where I lived. The neighbor down the street from me grew small amounts of marijuana that we would smoke and then satisfy our munchies with the fruit, sodas, and candy stolen on our heists. This further eroded my moral compass, and I soon began engaging in more serious behaviors – drinking alcohol, doing methamphetamine, stealing cars, and committing other types of criminal activity.

I committed a burglary at fourteen and was arrested in the act. The officers booked me into Juvenile Hall. My punishment was placement in a group home for boys where I stayed off and on for the next three years. I did well in the structured environment of the group home. It was a ranch-like setting in Calaveras County, CA, and I loved it. It felt like I was a part of a large family.

A couple of years after I was there, I was allowed to go to the public school in town and adjusted well to being in a more public and social setting. I was then allowed to go into a foster home where I had even more freedom.

I did, however, begin to drink alcohol on a regular basis. It made me feel "right," not so shy and afraid. I was drinking three or more times a week. I had a job in a grocery store and was stealing the alcohol from there. I was soon caught and kicked out of my foster family's house. I returned home to my parents' house and began running around with the neighbor kid down the street doing drugs, stealing, and getting into trouble. Before long, I was sent back to the group home for committing another burglary. By this time, my drinking and drug use had escalated. It was soon out of control, and I was kicked out of the group home right before my eighteenth birthday and sent back to Juvenile Hall.

A Troubled Man

I was released from Juvenile Hall on my eighteenth birthday after serving a week. I immediately contacted my family and asked them for help. My stepdad gave me a car – a bright yellow Volkswagen Beetle – and helped me get into a place to live near where I was going to attend college.

I did not stay in college long. I thought I needed to catch up on all the fun I felt I had missed out on during high school. The summer and winter of 1988 was one party after another – I drank and got high as often as I could. I was soon a full-blown addict and alcoholic. I lived on the streets, in and out of jail, and for the next five years immersed myself further and further into criminality. All that mattered was feeding my addiction. I stole from and lied to friends, family, and strangers. I used every angle I could to get what I felt like I needed. People became objects to use for my needs.

My early twenties were an extremely difficult part of my life. I began to experience an inner conflict regarding my sexuality – one I was not really aware of at the time. It was confusing and one of the main reasons for my drug addiction. The abuse I suffered as a young boy was not always unpleasant and, while it sickened me inside, my body often responded positively to it. As I got older, I sometimes felt a compulsion to place myself in situations with other men where the same abuse that had previously been perpetrated on me could be acted out – something that would make me feel victimized all over again. It began a cycle of despair and hopelessness that fueled deep seated anger and rage.

During this time, I had been traveling up and down the state stealing cars, doing burglaries, and committing other crimes. It was a pattern of jail, drug programs, then back to the streets to feed my addiction. On a few occasions when I was at my lowest lows, I prostituted myself for money to buy drugs. It was during one of these encounters on December 26, 1993, that I murdered a man.

I had never really been a religious person. I had been baptized as a Catholic when I was very young but was not really raised in the faith. My parents had been involved in various churches when I was younger. I went to church with them, but religion really wasn't practiced in our home with any regularity.

I had an idea though (a very Catholic one) that the murder I committed was a "Mortal Sin," one that would send me to Hell. I felt doomed and condemned by God. Prior to that night, I had felt like I was just a young man with a drug problem. Now I was a murderer waiting for God's judgment to fall upon me.

I went deeper into my drug addiction and at one point asked Satan to be the Lord of my life. I felt like God had already condemned me and that there was no turning back, so I might as well continue in the path of rebelliousness as far as I could.

God, however, had a different plan for me. I began to feel drawn to Christian literature and have a desire to know God. A few months after the killing, I was in jail again for another crime, and I asked to see a chaplain. I told him what I had done, and he asked me if I wanted to be forgiven. He explained the gospel to me, and I asked Jesus to come into my life. When I prayed with the chaplain, I felt a small outward tug in the center of my chest and then relief and peace washed over me. I felt free and at ease for the first time in my life.

I didn't give much thought to turning myself in for the crime, and it took twelve years for the murder to catch up to me. However, I never forgot what I had done. It weighed deeply on my soul, and I allowed it to drive me deeper into drugs and criminal behavior.

Between 1993 and 2004, I served five separate prison terms for various crimes. I was only out of prison for a total of about twelve months throughout those eleven years. I started out in the lower levels of the prison system and eventually spent time in every level of the prison system from fire camp to the Pelican Bay SHU.

My behavior in prison during these years was increasingly more violent and rebellious including staff assaults, cell extractions, riots, batteries, etc. Even so, I never prostituted myself again and never committed another robbery as the brutality and weight of murdering a man during a robbery kept me from doing something that could lead to the same result.

If life seemed difficult for me as a boy, it was hell during the years between the time I committed the murder and the time I was arrested for it. I fought loneliness and depression on a regular basis. I wanted to die and yet was too afraid to kill myself. When I was in prison, I would tell myself I would change when I got released. I never had a plan for how to change. It was just a dream I would always put off till later.

I never looked at the underlying reasons for my behavior. I would get out of prison, get a job, a place to stay, and then would relapse into addiction and criminality almost immediately. Frustration, anger, rage, and despair were constant companions who could only be silenced by the mind-numbing influx of any drug I could get my hands on.

I never really talked about the things that happened to me as a young boy. I hid them deep inside. I never made the connections between the abuse, my sexuality, the drug use, and the growing rage. Drugs and sex were compulsive behaviors covering up a severe and growing rage that I was unable to cope with. I thought that my difficulties with my sexuality were signs that I must be gay, but I have since realized that the confusion I experienced was directly related to the sexual abuse I endured as a young boy and couldn't share with anyone. These behaviors were driven by secrets that kept me in a cyclical pattern, roaring through life bent on destroying myself, hurting others, and escaping reality.

In November of 2004, I was ready to completely give up. I had been high on methamphetamine for several days and was contemplating getting a gun and committing suicide by cop. I was tired of hurting all of the people I loved, and I saw no way out of the addiction that had consumed me for so many years.

Before I could take any action on those destructive thoughts, however, I was arrested for auto theft and possession of burglary tools and placed in the Stanislaus County Jail.

While I was sitting in a chair in the county jail waiting to go to prison, the thought occurred that I had almost no desire for God, and that scared me. *What if I never had another desire for God again? What if the only person who brought me solace was never part of my life again?* I began to reach out to God, and soon He answered my prayers.

I began going to Bible studies and services. My attitude began to change very quickly. I started to realize that I could be free from my past and began to open up about my abuse in a way that started to bring freedom from guilt and shame. Seeing the impact that sharing some of my story with another person had was so powerful for me that I wanted to continue having that positive effect on other people. I intended to open up a Christian men's home when I was released.

On August 22, 2005, however, while I was still in jail, I was arrested for the murder I had committed in 1993. I had left DNA on cigarette butts and beer cans, and I was connected to the crime after new testing methods had been developed. During the interview with the detectives, I remember asking for an attorney and going back to a cell. In the cell, I laid on the floor feeling like I had had the wind knocked out of me. My life was over, and yet, I had a certain measure of calm.

I told God that I would not lie to get out of trouble, I would not manipulate the evidence to get a better outcome, I would not lie to my attorney, and I would not put the man's family through a trial. I just asked God to take care of my daughter and help me to honor Him.

I spent four years in the Santa Clara County Jail waiting for a resolution. During that time, I began to develop a closer relationship with the Lord. I had no TV or radio, just a few Christian books and my Bible. In 2008, I pled guilty to first degree murder and received a twenty-five year to life sentence. I was soon transferred to prison to begin doing my time.

A Kind God

Starting my life sentence was difficult. At that time in California a life sentence was a LIFE SENTENCE. People were not being released who had been convicted of murder. I was afraid that I would never go home and therefore the temptation to lie and get out of going to prison had been very strong. There were no witnesses, no weapon, and while they proved I had been at the crime scene, there was no proof that I had done anything. I had had a good chance of winning the case had I gone to trial, but I felt I would have lost something precious with God if I would have lied to go home. I chose to trust that God would either set me free one day or that He would surround me with His presence and make me happy to be wherever I was.

I showed up at the Deul Vocational Institute in Tracy, California, one of the CDC Reception

Centers, in June of 2009. I was dispirited. The weight of a life sentence was an Atlas-like burden that I did not think I could bear. I thought of suicide a few times and tried it once after I finally looked at photographs of the murder I had committed.

During the first couple of years in prison, I struggled with using, drinking, and other behavior issues. It was nothing like the violence that had been so common in my earlier prison terms, but significant nonetheless.

In 2011, I had a conversation with a Lieutenant at one of my disciplinary hearings. There was a lot of dysfunction happening on that particular prison yard and he asked me why I wasn't part of the solution. I didn't have an answer, but I had a strong conviction from God that I needed to quit feeling sorry for myself and begin living for Him.

I knew I was a Christian, but my life's actions did not match up to my convictions. I remember reading a book by Jerry Bridges called *The Pursuit of Holiness*. It detailed what holiness is and why it is necessary for Christians to pursue it. The book had a profound effect on me, and after reading it, I almost quit wanting to be a Christian! I felt like a lifelong pursuit of holiness filled with failure after failure to achieve the goal was a hopeless endeavor. I knew I could never be holy like God was calling me to be.

For a while, I was in a state of despair. I tried to be holy. I tried to quit selling pills and making wine to sell to provide for my needs. But I couldn't. The draw for material things was too much for me. I had alienated myself from my family and friends; I was in prison alone, for life, forever. I was even mad at God at times as if it was His fault that I had this struggle.

One day I was in my cell and during a prayer time had a thought that "God understood my dilemma" – that He was not mad at me for selling pills and making wine to meet my needs. Immediately it was like alarm bells were going off in my head. I knew that that was not true and if I chose to believe that lie, I would not be worshiping the God of the Bible but some god I was making up in my own little mind.

I began to cry and begged God to help me. I opened up to Him and told Him that I loved the things I could get with the pills and wine more than I loved Him and that I would always feel that way unless He changed my heart. I was afraid to die in prison alone, and I was afraid to live in prison alone. It was at my lowest point since being arrested for the murder.

Thankfully, God answered my prayer. He very suddenly gave me a sense of His presence, and in a flash, I had a purposeful desire to serve God and live my life to please Him. I began to pray more and read my Bible more. Once again, I told everyone I was not using drugs anymore, something I had done many times before and failed at. I got rid of all my pills, poured out my wine, and threw away my syringe. I didn't really know if this time would be different, but I was willing to do my best. That was in December of 2012.

Shortly after, I received a personal care package from a pastor in Texas to whom I had been writing for a while. I did not ask for the package; he just said that God had put it on his heart to send it to me. I felt like God was telling me in an intensely personal way that if I would just trust Him and be obedient, He would take care of my needs. I received a package every quarter after that for the rest of my time in prison. I never made wine again, I never sold pills again, and I stayed sober from drugs and alcohol for over ten years. God is faithful.

As I began to more intensely study my Bible, seek God, and obey Him, old behaviors and attitudes receded and new ones took their place. I slowly became a different person. I found out that holiness is not something that I earn or produce by my actions – it is something that is imputed to me on the basis of what Christ Jesus has done, and it manifests in my thoughts and actions as I honor God and obey him. The personal change was slow but steady.

Looking back, I can't point to a single day or time when I was "changed," but the day I prayed honestly to God and admitted to Him that I would not be able to change without His direct intervention was the beginning of a deep and lasting shift. I spent a lot of time in the chapel, I began teaching Bible studies and preaching sermons on the yard, and I spent a lot of time encouraging others to turn away from destructive lives and turn toward Jesus.

Sometime around 2014, laws began to change and lifers began to be released. I saw a few people go home but was pretty skeptical for myself. I still felt like I would never be released and that I would die in prison. A part of me was ok with that. Sometimes I felt like a wild dog that needed to be kept in a cage so that he would not hurt people. But another part of me desired to go home, to feel grass under my feet, and see a sunset that did not include concrete and razor wire.

As I saw more people go home, I began to have more hope that I could go home as well. I knew that I had changed and was no longer a danger to society, but the Board of Parole Hearings does not simply trust biblically-based change that does not incorporate evidence-based treatment methodologies. So, in addition to teaching Bible studies and serving in the chapel, I began to get involved in more programs such as Anger Management, Alternatives to Violence, Substance Use Disorder Treatment, and Criminal Thinking classes. I also took a lot of college courses.

I had my first parole hearing in January of 2021. I was denied parole for three years, but the commissioners gave me a clear road map of what I needed to do in order to earn a parole grant. Twelve months later, the Board reviewed my progress toward the things they had asked me to do and felt that I had done enough to warrant a new parole hearing. A hearing date was set for September of 2022, eighteen months earlier than I expected. God is faithful.

Freedom on the Outside

On September 29, 2022, I appeared before the Board of Parole Hearings for a second time. I was pretty nervous. After almost two hours of intense scrutiny of my entire life, including how I became a man who could murder a fellow human being and why it was reasonable to believe I was no longer a danger to society, the board recessed to deliberate my case. They deliberated for almost thirty minutes. It was the longest thirty minutes of my life.

Once the hearing restarted, the presiding commissioner said, "Based on the legal standards and the record, we find that you do not pose a current unreasonable risk to public safety and are, therefore, suitable for parole. So, Mr. Scheinuck, this is a grant of parole. The panel has found you suitable."

I didn't think I heard him right. I almost asked him to repeat what he had said, but instead I just waited, in disbelief. The commissioner began to give the reasons for the panel's decision. That's when I realized I was actually going to be allowed to go home. On some level, I still thought I would die in prison and would not ever be released.

I didn't really hear a lot after that. I was stunned. I had prepared to be released, I had done all of the work to be released, and I was no longer the same man who committed the atrocious murder; but I was still in shock that I was actually going home.

After the hearing ended, I just sat in the room and cried. The officer came in and asked what happened. "I was granted parole," I said.

I could tell that she was a bit confused about my tears. I explained that it was a bittersweet moment. I was happy that I would get to go home, but the man I murdered is still dead. His family is still grieving over his absence, and they will always be suffering. I still think about that almost every day.

I was released from custody on March 31, 2023, after serving seventeen and a half years on a twenty-five to life sentence. When I pled guilty to murder, I chose to trust that God would either set me free one day or that He would surround me with His presence and make me happy to be wherever I was. He kindly did both. My time in prison was not always easy, but I always had a deep sense of God's presence and knowledge of His providential care of me. I was happy to rest in Him and trust that He was working out all things for my good and for His glory.

I have been out of prison now for almost four months, and there have been a lot of blessings poured out on me by my Father in heaven. He has surrounded me with people that truly desire to see me become a successful productive citizen, including a pastor and his wife who picked me up when I was released. They opened their home up to me, gave me necessities including clothing and a phone, and gave me numerous rides to get ID's. Without their selfless assistance, I would not be where I am today.

I have been able to begin a relationship with my beautiful daughter whom I had not seen in twenty-four years. I have a good job at Rise Up Industries where I am learning a trade that will help me support myself, and I am in a Department of Rehabilitation program that is preparing me to become a mechanical engineer. I have opportunities that I never dreamed of.

I wish I could say that there have been no mistakes or hiccups during this reintegration process, but there have been. I relapsed on July 3, 2023. I allowed myself to become distracted with work, school, and various other things. I did not pay attention to warning signs related to my recovery and drank two tall cans of beer. My decision-making process became clouded, and I then used a large amount of methamphetamine that was laced with fentanyl, which resulted in an overdose.

I was found on a street corner unresponsive and spent two days unconscious in the hospital. I should be dead or back in prison right now. But God has again granted me mercy, and I am not taking it for granted. I have taken appropriate measures such as getting a sponsor, working the steps, going to meetings regularly, and increasing my support network to make sure that I am fully committed to my recovery.

It has been hard to adjust to society. This is not the same world I left in 2004. It moves fast, and I struggle to use technology, interact with so many different people, and the sheer amount of choices I have to make sometimes seem overwhelming. But I know that I am not alone.

Not only am I aware of God's presence, I have an amazing support network that has been there for me in more ways than I can count. Rise Up is an amazing place to work and learn how to be a good citizen. They have embraced me and did not give up on me when I relapsed. They have stood by me, and I am extremely grateful to be a part of their reentry program. I have never had a job like this where I cannot wait to get up and go to work.

I am not exactly sure what the future holds for me. I am learning a trade and going to school so that I can prepare myself to have a career, but those are secondary to my main goal in life. They are simply a way to support myself while I do what is really on my heart. I want to preach the gospel. I want to live all of my life for the glory of God and in honor of all the people who have been hurt by my former lifestyle.

I will never forget that my previous lifestyle led me to a place where I could take the life of another human being made in the image of God. I will not forget how much suffering I have caused by a life not well lived. I will not forget that there are people who will never get relief from the loss of a loved one whom they will never see again. I will not forget that I do not deserve the freedom I enjoy.

My life is not my own. And I will spend it reaching out to others who are on the same path of destruction that I was on. If I can only affect a few people, even if I can only affect one person, then maybe there will not be another family grieving the loss of a loved one and my freedom will not be wasted.

Conclusion

I started life as a broken young boy who turned into a troubled man that had no hope. I was a man who could only see his own pain and misery and spent most of his life lashing out at a world that he felt was hostile and suffocating. I desperately want to live out my life as an example of what God can do with a man like that. I want to be used as an instrument of healing in the lives of others who have been affected by trauma. That healing comes through the gospel of Jesus Christ, and my life is dedicated to sharing it and discipling those who respond.

Rewriting the Ink

Rewriting the Ink

Afterword
Leslie A. Willis

Write. Delete. Write. Rephrase.
Elaborate. Condense. Clarify.
Write, rewrite, write.

The journey of writing and editing a story, let alone a book, isn't a straight line. The first draft is never the final draft. Rounds and rounds of editing go into the product before it is shared with the public eye in order to best convey the raw, emotional, vulnerable truths of our stories.

It can be daunting, especially for a new author. However, once the process is experienced, it starts to become familiar. We know what to expect and can prepare ourselves for the process, so maybe the next time won't seem as difficult or surprising. And we learn what works best so not as many edits are needed for the next chapter.

Just as edits and rewrites take place in storytelling, so, too, do re-dos take place in our everyday lives. Call them second chances, new opportunities, or do overs, the reality is, we're constantly making adjustments – and hopefully, learning from our mistakes.

Every move we make, every sentence we write, is a decision. One thing happens, we consider our options regarding how we could respond, and then we take action. We write our next line.

We learn – consciously and subconsciously – through our experiences and the outcomes of the decisions we make. Mistakes will happen, some big and some small; that's a fact of life. It's what we do after our mistakes that really matters.

And so, we act on opportunities for improvement. We change our thought patterns and learn to manage our emotions. As the authors of this book show, we can begin to right our wrongs with new actions and transformed behaviors. Along the way, we experience setbacks and unexpected breakthroughs. We struggle, we succeed; we shift and we grow.

In this way, we are constantly writing and rewriting our life's stories. While we can't erase the parts we don't like, we can choose to write the next paragraph, a new chapter, a different ending. We can choose to make amends and ensure we do not make the same mistakes again. We can begin to honor those we have harmed by changing our ways and contributing positively to society. We can link our story to others and support them in writing a more favorable journey for themselves as well. Our journey, our story, is enhanced when it is connected to each other.

*****

"I'm nervous. It's really going to be out there. My family doesn't even know some parts of my story," Joe told me as we wrapped up the final round of edits on his stories. "I'm honestly not sure how they will respond. But it's my truth, and I want to tell it."

I could sense his resolve to complete this project, even with these hesitancies. Despite being advised by others to focus on his recovery after his relapse,

Joe came back more determined than ever to finish what he had started.

"This is something I feel called to do. It's part of my recovery. I want to get my story out there because I do believe it can have a significant impact on others."

Every time I sit down with one of these authors and listen to their stories, I admire their bravery to share and am reminded of how important it is to tell these stories. We often don't know what parts of our stories will resonate with others, spark a new way of thinking, or offer an element of self-discovery or healing. And yet, in sharing our stories, we give voice to experiences that often go untold and invite others into a space of connection.

I am honored to walk alongside these men in this journey. In a way, finishing this book is really just the end of one chapter. Another is beginning.

As we took the final group photo for the book cover, Mike pulled everyone in, realizing in that moment that, "This is it, guys. We did it. We've finished our book."

For a moment, no one spoke as we took in the reality of his words and let it sink in. Mike smiled, saying again, "We did it."

It's an accomplishment worthy of celebration. And in their joy, the authors are already looking toward the next chapter of where they would like to distribute their book – juvenile halls and prisons, their college reentry programs, and to others who are teetering on the brink of gang involvement or incarceration. Not to mention their families and loved ones, youth groups, even schools, and *your* bookshelf.

These four men show us that we can learn from our mistakes and invite others to learn from our mistakes as well, in hopes that they will make different choices. We can be brave and vulnerable to share our full truths, ask for help when we need it, and accept help when it is offered. We can find moments to laugh, to love, to acknowledge our accomplishments, and to find joy in the everyday. All the while honoring our past and those we have hurt along the way.

Perhaps in reading these stories, the next person will realize that they're not alone, that someone has walked the path before them and has come out on the other side. Change is possible. It starts with a commitment to find the right mix of ingredients.

My hope for these remarkable individuals is that they continue to share their stories, continue to be brave and vulnerable and strong, and continue to believe in who they have become.

Thank you for joining us on this journey.

Book Discussion Questions

1. What moment(s) in the authors' stories stand out to you the most? How did the stories impact you? What surprised you? What emotions did you feel as you read the stories?

2. What did you learn or discover from reading this book? Is there something you would like to learn more about? If you could ask the authors anything, what would you ask?

3. What were the authors looking for that led them into gang life? What aspects of gang life helped to fulfill their needs? What needs might have still been missing? How do these needs compare to your own needs? In what other ways could these needs be met?

4. What were the contributing factors – internal and external – that led to the authors'

incarceration? In what ways were the authors victims of a dysfunctional system?

5. What generational harms – psychological and emotional traumas that build up over time and are passed down through generations – do you see in these stories? What generational harms (direct and/or indirect) may be present in your own personal life? What generational harms may exist for other identities (socioeconomic status, race, religion, ethnicity, immigration status, cultural, etc.) not explicitly included in these stories? How might it be possible to disrupt generational cycles of harm?

6. After Joseph was arrested for the murder, he chose to take responsibility for his actions and pled guilty. What role does accountability play in righting wrongs? What additional actions may need to be taken to make amends after a harm has occurred? When have you taken accountability for something you've done? What was the outcome?

7. Michael speaks of the ingredients that together create the right recipe for change. The recipe is unique to each person. What were the key ingredients that contributed to each author's changes and their commitment to getting and staying out of prison? What ingredients –

people, experiences, opportunities, beliefs – have contributed to your own progress and success in life?

8. What resources and support did the authors have during their reentry to help them stay out of prison? What support for individuals and communities could be put in place to disrupt the cycles of incarceration and recidivism? What support should be provided to young people specifically? In what ways should society be held accountable to protecting and supporting marginalized and underserved communities?

9. Several of the authors talk about freedom – freedom from authority, freedom from prison and violence, freedom of choice. Where do you see freedom in the authors' stories? What does freedom mean in your life? From where do you see yourself still desiring to break free?

10. Not all people are born with equal access to resources and opportunities. Where do you see societal inequities in these stories? In what areas of your own life have you experienced privilege or a lack thereof (e.g. zip code, race, ethnicity, socioeconomic status, gender, citizenship, etc.)? How has that status contributed positively or negatively to your life opportunities? What

world can you envision in which there is equity and equality for all people? How might we work together as a society to level the playing field for all?

11. These are human stories – raw, real, emotional. Where did you see a connection to yourself and your own life experiences in the lives of the authors? What differences did you notice? What assumptions did you hold about individuals who experience incarceration prior to reading these stories? After reading these stories, how has your knowledge or view changed?

12. What are ways you could get involved in your community to support individuals coming out of prison or to prevent individuals from turning to gangs or going to prison in the first place? What programs and resources already exist in your community? Where do you see areas for improvement? What would you like to learn more about?

Resources

The following is a list of national hotlines and resources in the USA:

National Suicide Prevention Lifeline
Call 988

National Domestic Violence Hotline
1 (800) 799-7233

RAINN National Sexual Assault Hotline
1 (800) 656-4673

Childhelp National Child Abuse Hotline
1 (800) 422-4453

Substance Abuse and Mental Health Services Administration National Helpline
1 (800) 662-4357

Gay, Lesbian, Bisexual and Transgender National Hotline
1 (888) 843-4564

Alcoholics Anonymous
AA.org

Narcotics Anonymous
NA.org

Unsure where to start?
Call 211, the National Human Service Call Center, for assistance.

Acknowledgments

We want to extend a collective thanks to many individuals whose support made this book possible:

To Joe Gilbreath and the staff at Rise Up Industries – namely Dustin, Darren, Nicole, and Jonathan – for supporting each step to make this book a reality, seeing the benefits of this process, and giving us valuable work time to complete this project.

To the individuals who did an initial read of the book and contributed to the editing process, especially Robin, Laura, and Debi.

To Ernie Garcia for writing the Foreword and continuing to give back to the community and Rise Up Industries.

To everyone who donated to our fundraiser to support the initial costs of publishing and printing this book.

To our families who have supported us through this project and through so much more.

Individually, there are a few people each author would like to thank and acknowledge, individuals who have been integral in their lives both during and beyond the writing of this book:

Michael – I would like to thank my wife, my parents, my brother, my in-laws, my children, and my grandson. I would also like to acknowledge Lori Warren from RedF, Yohanny Conona-Batalona from Justice Scholars, Dr. Mobley from Project Rebound, Dr. Reese from the Prison Education Project, and Jesse Martinez for being my truest friend.

Frank – I would like to thank my mom Anita for never giving up on me, my wife Dulce for giving me the spark to continue to push forward, and my Parole Officer Ms. Flores for strongly encouraging me to get this job at Rise Up Industries.

Jesse – I would like to thank my family and my girl for pushing me to stay on this path and this new way of life.

Joseph – I would like to acknowledge and thank the following people for their support and commitment to my success: Prison Fellowship Regional Director Pam Gonzalez, Pastor Danny Gonzales, Suzanne Bueno at Pathways to Success, Diana Vidrio at Second Chance, Pastor Les Walthers, Pastor Martin Dawson, my friend Steven Gonzales, RUI Program Manager Mike Lucero, and RJ Donovan Protestant Chaplain Amy Campbell.

Without the assistance, love, and care of these individuals, we would not be where we are today.

And to you, our readers, thank you for listening to our stories with an open mind and an open heart, a willingness to explore other walks of life, and the compassion to see the humanity in each of us.

The Authors

Jesse Avina

Michael Lucero

Frank Perez

Joseph Scheinuck

About the Project

This book is the second book written by members of Rise Up Industries' Reentry Program in San Diego, California. The storytelling project that ultimately culminated in the first publication, *Writing After Life,* was started in February 2018 by the editor, Leslie Willis, in collaboration with Rise Up Industries employees, as part of her Master of Arts in Social Innovation capstone project. *Rewriting the Ink* is a continuation of this project.

By sharing stories, this project provides the opportunity for individuals to explore and take ownership of their experiences, to feel empowered to use their voices to heal, and to create connections and understanding between people of different walks of life.

Rewriting the Ink is a product of the journey the authors and the editor took together and now invite others to join. It is a journey of discovering, first and foremost, our common humanity.

A Word from the Founder of Rise Up Industries

Joe Gilbreath

I applaud the authors' courage to openly share their life stories. It is sad to hear about the challenges they experienced so early in their lives. But it is also inspiring to hear about their courage to embrace their experiences, to change their lives, and to help others.

Rise Up Industries is celebrating its 10-year anniversary in 2023. Our 18-month Reentry Program – that all four authors have enrolled in – is in its eighth year of serving the previously incarcerated population. While each member coming through our program is a unique individual with his own history, one thing that is common to all is that they didn't start life on a level playing field. They all faced significant challenges as youth. They often did not have the guidance or the experience to face these significant challenges. Yet at some point in their later adulthood, they came to recognize a deeply rooted basic human desire of wanting the best for others. This has led them to change their lives, in spite of many obstacles, and to make amends, give back, and help others.

Many of our program members and graduates, including several of these authors and those of *Writing After Life*, have been involved in speaking engagements with at-risk youth. Their message to the youth is that they have value and self-worth. They encourage these youth to recognize and embrace their value and to avoid the paths that they experienced.

Rise Up Industries is preparing to launch its Rise Up Leadership Academy that will serve our San Diego community's at-risk youth who are facing many of the same challenges that our Reentry Program members faced in their youth. Through sharing their stories, our Reentry Program members and graduates are helping us to understand the needs of these youth. Many will be involved as credible messengers, helping the youth to recognize their value, to successfully navigate the challenges they face, and reach their full potential.

Finally, I am grateful for the initiation of Leslie Willis in assisting Rise Up Industries' members in writing their stories. Benefits of this project is a two-way street. Reflecting and writing about one's life helps the writer recognize and then release attachments to the trauma of his past. At the same time, the sharing of their stories is an inspiration for others to see that change in their lives is also possible. And finally, it raises community awareness of the critical needs of our at-risk youth, and the consequences if these needs are not met.

Did these stories inspire you? Stay connected with Rise Up Industries:

Tour the Training Center in San Diego

Donate

Volunteer

Follow us on Instagram or Facebook

Sign up for our Quarterly Newsletter

For more information, go to
riseupindustries.org/get-involved
or email info@riseupindustries.org.

Made in the USA
Monee, IL
03 September 2023

42051560R00095